My Medicine
POETRY & SHORT STORIES
CHARISSA

Books may be purchased by contacting the publisher and author at:
hello@penwings.com
Cover Design: Charissa Ong Ty
Illustration: Adrianus Harris
Publisher: Penwings Publishing
Editor: Penwings Publishing
ISBN: 978-967-14227-9-3
1. Poetry 2. Fiction
First Edition

Printed by:
Percetakan Okid Sdn Bhd
No. 2, Jalan SS 13/3C, Subang Jaya Industrial Estate,
47500, Subang Jaya, Selangor, Malaysia.

Published by: Penwings Publishing
Subang Jaya, Selangor Darul Ehsan, Malaysia.

Contents

*Disclaimer: The author in no way approves any misuse of drugs or alcohol. If you are experiencing any mental health challenges or body discomfort, please take time out of your schedule to visit a health professional.

Today was the day I fell in love with poetry once more.

I didn't simply just write them. Instead, I let the words float freely downstream from my heart into the void before me. The broken letters rearranged themselves in perfect order, as if it were sheet music ready to be played by a concerto. It was beautiful. With nervous anticipation I read the notes and hummed the sad tune softly, careful not to stir the water. And in the still reflection, I see me.

My poetry.

Blue pills

Romantic comedies

I'd switch it on and cast us as the leads,
as it was fairly easy to do,
for she was a little bit like me,
and he was a little bit like you.

Fate would bring us to a bookstore,
one tucked in a little corner by the shore.
Our love story would quicken,
and the plot would thicken,
driving us further away than before.

I won't see you for another 6 months,
understood well,
that fate only happens once.

But, by a stroke of luck,
fate decides that we were to be wed,
and I'll watch us have,
the happy ever after we never had.

Underwater

I cried myself a river,
because everything is quieter underwater.

Signs

I tried writing your name in the sand,
but the waves wouldn't let me.
I shaped your name with twigs and leaves,
but the breeze tossed it back into the sea.

Then I carved your name into an old tree,
but it only made my fingers cut and bleed.
Was it nature's way of telling me,
that I should forget you completely?

I told you I loved you,
every time we waved goodbye,
but you always replied with a
faint air of boredom and a lie.

I dreamed of a future,
where there would only be you and I,
but you'd remind me to live in the present,
and to stop asking —
why.

Scars

You're a scar,
I don't mind talking about.

Goodbye letters

"Write a goodbye letter. It'll help you with your sorrow."
There were 238 letters ever since, and one more tomorrow.

Wendy Darling

You're all grown up, darling Wendy,
why didn't you wait for me?
You gave your heart away, Wendy,
to a grown-up and a little baby.

My heart hurts, Wendy,
wasn't that kiss only for me?

I love you, Wendy,
but you loved growing up,
more than you ever did me.

Wanderer

Wondrous wandering wanderer,
what and where art thou wondering?
Shalt thy feet lure thyself further,
vow, that thy heart would always,
wander home to me.

Are you my fairy?

There once was a boy,
who fell in love with a girl.
The girl did not love him back,
it was the end of his world.

Then, one day,
the boy falls in love with a fairy.
And the fairy loved him back.
This made the girl jealous,
she wanted the boy back.

The boy left the fairy.
The fairy never sees herself as a fool,
it hurts too much to be known as a tool.
She tells herself that she's a fairy,
and the hurt that comes,
is sometimes necessary.

As long as the boys she loves,
are good and happy,
love will exist,
and so will this fairy.

Volumes

My actions spoke volumes,
but he didn't know how to read me.

12

Love sick

The air around me grew thicker,
making it hard to breathe.

My heart breaks into a fever,
my soul weakens to its disease.

Love can make you stronger,
but it can also make you sick.

To the moon

I love you to the moon and back,
and even more than that.

I'll love you,
even if you don't love me back.

Learn to be lonely

I loved you enough to let you go,
sacrificed the joy of all my tomorrows.
There's nothing you can do to help me,
for I have to learn to be lonely.

15

The fault in our stars

Every day I hope and pray,
that our stars will align one day.
If our stars have aligned before,
it could do it again once more.

For certain

I don't know,
if you are ever coming home.

I don't know,
how long I'll be okay alone.

I don't know,
If I'm ever going to look into the eyes
that tell me I'm loved again,

Or be surprised,
by Eskimo kisses in the rain.

The uncertainty goes on,
another night, another dawn,
but there's one thing I'm certain,

Is that my love for you,
continues to burn.

Shooting stars

I made a wish on seven shooting stars,
wished with all my heart and hoped,
by some miracle, we'd go far—
Oops! Missed a few,
my eyes were closed.

We'd climb every mountain,
explore old streets and bars.
In a world that's so uncertain,
we'd stay true to who we are.

And when it's time,
we'll leave this world.
And by some miracle,
we'd go far,
we'll float our hearts upward,
til we're one,
with the stars.

It's raining

Empathetic clouds,
cry with me.

They thunder loud,
shrouding me.

I think of you,
and cry some more.

Every day,
it pours and pours.

Infected

The warmth of your love,
is nothing but a fantasy.
It was more like a fever,
destroying me slowly.

More alone

I feel more alone now,
than I've ever been.

You have amplified the silence,
and reduced me from deep within.

My skin feels colder than it was before,
the warmth in my smile,
is no more.

I need you

I need you to be there for me always.
I need you to be there for me.
I need you to be there.
I need you to be.
I need you.

Love me, if you can.

Remember me as I am, my love,
when you could see my soul through my eyes,
and hear the love in my voice when I call out your name.

Don't cry,
when I can't recognize your touch anymore,
or know that you need a hug
when you're curled up on the floor.

Read me my stories and poetry,
and I'll try my hardest to come back to you.
I'll love you back wholeheartedly,
even if it's just for a little while...

I'm sorry, but do I know you?

Shoes

On the day you walked away,
I tried to put myself in your shoes.
I wore them every single day,
until I didn't want me too.

Probability

1. The right person, the wrong time, at the wrong place.
2. The right person, the right time, at the wrong place.
3. The right person, the wrong time, at the right place.
4. The wrong person, the right time, at the wrong place.
5. The wrong person, the right time, at the right place.
6. The wrong person, at the wrong time, at the right place.
7. The wrong person, at the wrong time, at the wrong place.
8. The right person, at the right time, at the right place.

1. Puppy love
2. Long-distance relationships
3. In love with someone who's taken
4. One night stands
5. Unhealthy, abusive relationships
6. One-sided love affair
7. Strangers
8. True love

Playboy

My lonely, reserved heart is my peril,
for I will not settle.

So all I do now is love parts of you
in every other woman, until I find you.

Roses

Bouquet in hand, he squeezes his way into the crowded train, protecting its fragile petals.

Who were they for?

He looks at them and a tiny smile escapes his lips.

Who did he love?

Nervous for an anniversary dinner or a second date, he fidgets with his hair and taps rhythmically on the handrail. Like those flowers, he hoped she could see their love bloom into something more. She'd receive those flowers, look into his grey eyes, kiss him and reassure him that he's loved. Without a pause, he'd kiss her smile and tell her how lucky he is to be loved by her. A ding escorts me back from my make-believe narrative.

He alights the train, along with the stories he never shared.

In her own time

Time is an important currency,
for there is no time for ambiguity.

Tell me you love me, baby,
and I'll be yours in a heartbeat.

I'll give you all of my seconds,
hours, minutes and weekends,
Invest in our love daily.

But please, whatever you do,
do not lead me astray, my lady.

Ships

Poets fantasize about a new friendship,
that moves quickly into a courtship.
It's challenged by a trickle of hardship,
then gracefully ends in a beautiful relationship.

But,
these trips are making her sick,
wondering if there's a tip or trick.
Oh, how she yearns for her own shore,
more and more.

Smoke and fog

You were a mystery,
I couldn't decipher.
Were you the one for me?
I wasn't sure.

You fanned the flame,
and it drove me insane.
Was it a signal?
Or another riddle?

Mind clouded,
I followed the source,
choking and deluded,
you weren't there,
of course.

30

Remember why

"Do you remember why you came back for me?" she asked.
"I... can only remember the reason I left in the first place," he answered.
"Then, there is no more reason for you to stay," and she left.

Vessels

Love happens,
when two are in love.

Love is created from nothing,
and stored in vessels for sharing.

Emptiness is properly cared for,
when these vessels tip and pour,
back and forth into one another,
forever filling each other.

However,
if one vessel empties itself constantly,
while the other stays full abundantly,
their love would run dry eventually.

The full vessel will be unable to comprehend,
what it's like to be empty; it reaches a dead end.

32

I left

I fell in love with you with every passing day,
but I knew you were never going to stay.

So I said Goodbye to you before you knew,
how much I needed you in every single way.

I'm sorry

"I'm so sorry, I've had some time to think about us and I realised that you were... are my everything," her past choked.

"I'm sorry, but I've realised that I can't-"

"Babe, who's there at the door?" her future asked.

"An old friend," she answered.

The door shuts, leaving her past and future at the porch.

"Hey man, I've heard a lot about you," said her future, as he folded his arms tight across his chest.

"...What did she say?" her past asked.

Her future sighs.

"I don't know how to say this... but I need to thank you. Thank you for setting her free. If you hadn't, I wouldn't have had the chance to be a part of her future. I'm very much in love with her like you are right now. But the only difference is that you've had your chance. I'm sorry."

Are you even my friend?

Take time out of your life,
to listen to me.
I have problems,
let's talk about it.

I said 'Hi' to you,
so that we could talk about me.

It's not about you,
it's about me.

Oh, you're busy?
time to refocus your focus,
back to me.

Aren't you worried about me?
do you even know,
how a friend should be?

35

He knows

He was able to break your heart and destroy you,
only because you've trusted him enough to tell him,
exactly how to do it.

Hello, Dad.

It has been 27 years,
since you've been gone,
I've never met you,
but life still went on.

She doesn't talk much-
about you at all,
except for that one day,
when she breaks protocol.

She feels like she owes it to me,
to manage her grief when she recalls-
every happy memory,
or anything of you at all.

To have so much love for someone-
who doesn't exist anymore,
I guess it's still possible,
to love someone,
I've never met before.

1000 nights

I'd rather bear the emptiness of a thousand nights,
than to be full, then crushed into nothing on a single night.
With an empty shell, there's still space to fill,
but a shattered vessel loses its identity and will.

You left

You left me alone to think about us.
You left me alone to think.
You left me alone.
You left me.
You left.

Distance

They say that absence makes the heart grow fonder,
but all his heart ever did was wander.

I write to feel

I write to feel,
when nothing hurts me anymore.

I write in desperate need,
to feel something more.

I write to remember,
how feelings feel like, long before.

Stories sealed in dead stars,
are but old, pretty twinkles
you adore.

41

Remember us

Remember us even if it hurts your heart.
Remember us even if it hurts you.
Remember us even if it hurts.
Remember us.
Remember.

Never like that

Was she insecure?
She was never like that.

Jealous?
She was never like that.

Dependent?
She was never like that.

Emotional?
It's okay to be like that.

Was she emotionally unstable though?
She was never like that.

But with you,
she was always like that.

Never-ending

All broken hearts were once whole,
and all whole hearts were once broken.
This cycle of breaking and mending,
never ceases, it's never-ending.

Burden

I hope you never find your perfect person,
God forbid if you ever lose them.

Best to be left naive and uncertain,
for finding someone as perfect,
can be quite a burden.

tree

*

Hey,

~*~*~

check out,

~*~*~*~*~*~

this little Xmas

~*~*~*~~*~*~*~~*~

tree I wrote into existence.

~~*~*~*~~*~*~*~~*~*~*~*~

Now, if only it'll work the same

way with

your name.

Her eyes are not yours

It's our daughter's 57th birthday today, honey.

She asked me if I still loved you, and in a heartbeat, I told her, "I most definitely do, because mama lives in my heart all the time!"

She loved that answer.

But to tell you the truth, my heart breaks every time I look into her eyes because I see you there all the time. She has your eyes, but it isn't yours.

At times I would find myself searching for you there, but those eyes did not hold our secrets. I remember the day I kissed you by the lake, the day you said you loved me back, and the day we said I do. It's a pity, that there is no one else to remember these memories differently.

"Grandpa, what are you thinking about?"

"Oh, it's nothing, Clara. What do you want to talk about?"

I replied, heartbroken once again as I stared into another empty vessel that resembled yours.

47

me

It's just me and you against the world.
It's just me and you.
It's just me.

Storyteller

I don't have to be a part of your future,
to be with you,

Take me on your adventures,
and I'll take you on mine too.

Turn me into your favorite tale,
one with risks and danger,
don't forget the little details,
like the jokes and banters.

Tell them about the friendship that never failed,
and about the love that almost prevailed.

They would ooh and ahh, cry and sing,
when our story ends more beautifully,
than its beginning.

Wounds

Time may not heal all wounds of the broken.

But for some,
it is a measure of how long they can stay open.

I release you

You deserve to be free,
it's alright, if it's not with me.

Love of mine,
gleam and glow,
let your colors shine.

Although your tears may stream,
light a lamp for your dreams.

Through summers and winters,
I'll watch over you and remember,
your love for me,
and mine for you,
forever.

Petals

He loves me, he loves me not,
will never be a thought,
for he loves me so surely,
it left no room for obscurity.

-

She loves me, she loves me not,
I'll continue hoping,
although she does not.

She's just a convenience

"I would never change my world for one person.
There's always someone else for me wherever and whenever I am."

"But she isn't just someone, is she? She's not just a person but your
entire world. Are you really ready to let her go? Because if you do,
there is no turning back. You'll spend an eternity searching for
ghosts of her in every woman, but they will never be truly, her."

Lost boy

You found me,
and I found you.
You loved me,
then I lost you.

When you think of me in the middle of the night,
with tears falling, your chest tight,
look for me in the second star to the right.

I'll be looking for a star to its left too,
heartsick, arms aching to hold you.

Nobody

For a person who writes so much about love,
she sure spends a lot of time avoiding it.

Why,
the more she talks about it, the less she understands it,
her soul burns for it, but she never lets just any flame consume her spirit.

She overthinks it, or doesn't think about it at all,
"There's probably no one out there," she admits,
nobody for her, nobody at all.

Drugs

"Don't do it man, it's not worth it. Your heart beats
weird, you get giddy, stupid even. You'll really lose
yourself. Don't get me started on the withdrawals."

"How do you get it?"

"True love? It's extremely hard to come by
and we're lucky it is."

You're mine only

Who is she? Is she a new friend?
I'm afraid I'll lose a best friend,
if I let you fall in love with her.

Please, anyone but her.

We're the perfect pair,
I've always been there,
I'll reduce her existence,
to a temporary occurrence.

She won't have enough time,
to be important enough in your life.

'It's not worth getting to know her.'
'Both of you will only get hurt.'
'I know how girls are, they'll always want more.'
'It's always best friends before wh*res.'

'You'll ruin everything, and this.'
'Don't see her, pinky promise?'

I'll hammer these words hard into your brain,
again and again.

She might be the perfect one for you,
and everything you've been looking for,
but you don't need to learn that,
because I'm all you'll ever need and more.

Dreams your heart makes

I dreamt of you last night.
It was so pure and right.
I loved you so much in it,
and you loved me too.

I nestled into your arms,
like it's the most natural thing in the world,
and you hugged me so close,
it felt like you'd never let go.

We laid there for a while,
and you told me you loved me with just your eyes,
kissed my brow, nose, and hair between smiles.

The lump in my throat told me,
that this heaven was just a dream my heart made,
because I knew that the moment we fell asleep,
it would all disappear as soon as I wake.

Oh, I'd fight in any war,
to hurt like this once more.

I've tried it all

It's been a year.
I should be okay by now.

I've tried giving myself time.
I've tried putting myself first.
I've tried being alone,
removed all physical memories,
and the number to your phone.

I've tried working in excess,
and working way less.
I've tried different hells,
I've pictured you with someone else.

I've tried therapy,
I've tried being around friends and family.
I've tried new hobbies that I thought were cool,
I've even tried being very grateful.

I've tried to ignore you,
I've even tried seeing someone new.
I've tried everything but nothing's working.

I've tried it all,
except running straight to you.

Where were you?

I looked for you in every chamber of my heart,
hoping that you still made yourself at home here.

But I found a letter instead,
filled with words that hit me like a dart.

It read,
'You don't need me anymore, you didn't seek me for over a year.
It's okay to be happy, have no fear;
don't be afraid to make room for someone else, my dear.
I'll always be with you and I love you.
Cheer up now, and wipe those tears.'

Fate

Fate led you to me,
but it also took you away.

Fate has then made you free
to stay away or to stay.

She still takes it

I shouted my secrets to the sky,
and the moon acknowledged them with a smile.
I breathed a loving response into the wind,
and the rain washed the dirt off my skin.

I thank her for sustaining such abuse,
from parasites concerned only with luxury and use.

It's a wonder, despite the strain,
the earth loves us, ignores it all,
and takes it all over again.

One out of a thousand

I've penned thousands of poems,
tucked in between thousands of books,
over the seas and skies, they roam,
a millennia of inspiration they took.

I've written songs decorated with a thousand melodies
carved from a thousand emotions.
I've written plays with one actor,
and plays with a thousand more,
adorned with acts of adventure, and unselfish devotion,
a take on a private play performed; starring us, long before.

I sit here alone, wishing,
praying that you still knew how much I loved you,
hoping that just one out of the thousands,
had made its way to you.

Used

She built herself
with my broken pieces,
and made herself real,
by using all of my wishes.

With half of my heart gone

With half of my heart gone,
my blood pumps slower than before.

Everything is in slow motion,
as I lie here, on my bedroom floor.

With half of my heart gone,
my heart has lost its rhythm.

Emotions to calm or to quicken,
it doesn't know them.

With half of my heart gone,
half of the weight is lost,
an uneasy weightlessness,
no one can ignore.

With half of my heart gone,
I fill the empty crevice,
with should bes and could bes,
if half of my heart hadn't gone.

I still recreate you in my dreams

Have I subconsciously preserved your little quirks, gait, accent, and slurs long enough that even after twenty-three years, I could still recreate you? You'd ask me about your granddaughter and her predicament of choosing between music and accounting, and I'd recognize the softness in her eyes, filled with concern and love when I was at a similar crossroad. You frowned at the right moments and laughed at the wrong ones just like you used to; it's so unfair that only I could see you. Mother, you haven't aged a day. You've kept your promise, and you stayed.

I would, but not right now
I would, but not right now

I would love you to know that we're nothing more than casual.
I would love you to know that we're nothing more.
I would love you to know that we're nothing.
I would love you to know.
I would love you.
I would.

She can't leave

She knows that he loves other women,
but she can't leave.

She knows she isn't truly happy,
but she can't leave.

She knows that he will leave her,
but she can't leave.

She knows that she deserves better,
but she can't leave.

So, she rephrases her anxiety,
to make herself feel better, quietly.

She thinks it's okay for him to love more people,
and that happiness is just a state of mind,

Anxiety and insecurity are not for cool girls like her,
and that she's free to leave and love others,
although honestly, it will never occur.

'At least he's better than what I had before,'
is what she says, when doubt arises at her core.

So, she doesn't leave.

Her thought process begins all over again,
every minute, and every hour of every day,
for months and years,
and even on public holidays.

Denial

He tells her he loves her often,
to convince himself that he should.

On queue, her heart softens,
and filters in only the good.

Self regulation

She does not go to anyone
for her problems,
because everyone goes to her for theirs.

They take up all her time
telling her what they want to hear,
with no interest in doing right,
or facing their fears.

Not being honest is serious self-betrayal,
she can't imagine making someone else personally disloyal.

So she goes back alone,
to her quiet little corner and books,
rereads the script and replays the looks.

She then asks questions to
nobody in particular,
until someone else in her mind
wakes and answers.

There are pieces

The broken pieces of my heart found their home in the life we made. It's funny how they chose the oddest of places to lay.

There are pieces of you in the washing machine, with its high pitch chimes reminding me that our clothes are now clean, ready to be put away.

Sitting patiently in the cupboards are pieces of you in the clean dishes and pans, bracing themselves once again for our food experiment of the day.

I see us laughing, reflected in the almost finished honey jar. The Connoisseurs of Desserts, is what we said we were.

A large piece of you is lodged onto your half-used soap; just a few more baths and I will no longer smell like you, I hope. Just like the soap, memories of you should disappear gracefully, praying that time will be kind to me.

I left your side of the bed empty, not wanting to scatter the multitude of broken pieces piled up on your pillow. For under the right light of the stars, its shards reflect your beautiful, loving, honest eyes looking back at me once again, from not too long ago.

Red dress

She's a 10,
but she dons her red flags.

She credits the men,
who gave her the rags.

Fall

Fallen leaves,
crunched, but not seen,
chilly winds,
echo where you've been.

How I wish for a finer fellow,
warm, beautiful and as crisp,
as these browns, reds, and yellows;
someone who loves me all of today,
and a little bit more tomorrow.

Shattered but whole

She carved him up into beautiful little parts,
lighted a fire and pulverized his bones.

She broke his soul, all that he owned, and his heart,
and left him screaming into the dark,
alone.

But what she did not know,
was that by leaving him broken,
he could finally be whole,
on his own.

Anywhere, but there.

I have fantasies,
of meeting you in an old bookstore,
or at a friend's house party,
falling the moment you walk through the door.

I want to meet you anywhere,
just not there.

I want to meet you in a museum,
where you'd ponder for five to six minutes,
on pieces of art with the utmost decorum.
Eventually, you'd take me for a rare exhibit,
the only piece you are able to fathom.

I'd love to meet you,
anywhere, but there.

I dream of a charming smile on the train,
and the one I'd return as consent
for you to come share what you can't contain,
about the book I'm reading, before I went.

We would meet anywhere,
but there.

I want to meet you unrealistically, or none at all,
therefore, I'm afraid I would never meet you at all.

I want to hate you

But I can't.

The very thought of you,
disgusts me.

Loving you,
irks me.

I don't want to be your friend.
I hate your perfectly plump lips when—

I refuse,
fantasizing about your body
and how it collides desperately into mine,
leaving us in a tangled mess of limbs only
to satiate your soaring hunger with my—

No.

Take it away.
stop. STOP.

I'd do anything,
to hate you. But I can't.

Part of me wishes that you'd see me,
but a larger part of me,
wishes for you to be

happy.

Broken leaves

The broken hide their feelings from you.

Thus, to know how they were broken,
watch who they are kindest to.

For only with the presence of fallen leaves,
will you be able to see the shape of the wind
and know what it's going through.

Happy pills

Unspoken

You were a splash of yellow in my world of gray,
for you said words I'm too afraid to say.

You loved me with all the words you've ever known,
and I loved you back with all the actions I've shown.

"I love you always," my eyes and hugs would admit,
and you always knew,
although I hardly ever said it.

The girl who was everything

She who is in love with life and everything in it,
had boys falling in love in less than a minute.

Heart monitor

Why my belief in love
dies—,
I think of us.

And—⋀—in a heartbeat—
I believe again,
like it was my first.

82

Flowers

Instead of a bouquet,
you brought me to a field of flowers,
far, far away.

No longer did I remember *love* as devout possession till death,
but of freedom and a chance at a life worth every breath.

Lessons of love

You taught me,
that true love
could grow in silence,
and disagreements.

You taught me,
that anger can be understood,
broken down,
and used for good.

I've learned that love,
can be beautifully effortless,
and at the same time,
heartbreakingly perilous.

But most importantly,
you taught me,
that it's okay,
to be truly,
unapologetically,
me.

84

Aspire

I want a love that starts and ends the same way,
one of kindness, magic, and crazy stories we can't say.

Mortals

You should never love me as a God,
and I shan't pray to you as my hero.

We're both mortals on equal ground,
free souls, down the river we flow.

First sight

The winds boasted its color,
their echoes tasted sweet,
it led us to one another,
for our eyes to meet.

Love Language: Receiving Gifts

You're a different kind of materialistic,
a hopeless romantic, a little altruistic.
There's truth in physical representations,
these symbols of love prove my vocations.

Here's a little trinket to remember me by,
memories to make you smile; don't you cry.
Wear our love proudly on your finger,
a part of me is with you always,
now and forever.

Love Language: Acts of Service

Your efforts are proof that you love me,
for actions speak louder than words.
You make my life so easy,
In return,
I'll give you the love you deserve.

I'll cook your favorite stew,
and help you dry your hair.
I'll take you to that interview;
pluck confidence out of thin air.
These are just some of my silent dos,
to show you that "I love you."

Love Language: Quality Time

Quality time with you
is unparalleled to
any expensive gift,
love note or grand gesture.
If you give me a little of your time,
I'll pledge you all of mine.

-

Timeless views of Mt Fuji, or
impermanent cherry blossoms,
moments with you are all
everlastingly precious.

A poem collaboration with P.S.

Love Language: Physical Touch

His warmth protects me,
against my cold, delusional insecurities.

Without a word,
he wraps me in his arms securely,
and hugs away all my anxieties.

-

Her kisses are my addiction,
they are proof that she is real.

They're lovelier than any fantasy,
for I'm now healed.

Love Language: Words

You don't have to be suspicious.
Be assured that I love only you.
I'll plant words of love between kisses,
be a man of my word, my vow stays true.

I'll say to you,
'How was your day?'
'Sweet dreams, boo.'
'Are you okay?'
'You're so beautiful.'
They're just different ways,
I say *I love you.*

How do I know?

I knew that she was the one,
when I didn't have to lie
to impress.

I knew that she was my eternity,
when I didn't have to wait
or to guess.

But above all, I'll know she's mine,
when I didn't need to pretend,
to love her less.

Meeting the One

When you meet the one,
your heart does not beat faster,
your palms do not get sweatier.

Instead,
your breath is calmer,
her soul, familiar.

94

It's your turn, Mom.

Because tripping is less scary,
when you're on my team.

Now mom, focus on chasing your story,
it'll be nice to finally see your tired eyes gleam.

95

Don't tell me your dreams

It was a mistake for you to tell me your dreams,
for I'll do whatever it takes until you achieve it.
My time, love, and effort I'll sacrifice,
even though I could potentially be the price.

I'll protect you

When you're alone,
my time, I'll loan.
If he breaks your heart,
I'll restore it to the start.
When you're sad or mad,
I'll wipe the tears you shed.

You are my everything,
my world and my life,
and with a flap of my wings,
I'll take with me, your 16 years of strife.

You won't remember them too,
I'll watch over and protect you.
I hope I brought you love and joy,
because Momma always said,
I was a good boy.

True colors

I don't see why you'd hide your true colors from me,
for they're the most beautiful colors I've ever seen.
I could never choose to only love one shade of you,
when my world was in black and white,
before knowing you.

I'll bring heaven to you

I'll take you to a place far away so you could dance,
you'd turn to me and smile, making me fall at a glance.
Then we'll laugh under the rain and kiss in the trees,
Sit in comfortable silence, and enjoy the breeze.

Spoken for

My heart was already spoken for,
although he didn't say a word at all.

Magic flower

If you can find me and consume me,
you will live forever.

I would first taste sweet, sour, then bitter.
See me through the tinted glass,
for I'm more than just a magic flower.

Many left just before dusk,
but if you stay,
you'll see why I'm sought after.

I am fire,
I am love,
I am warmth and also your savior,
love me until it is all over,
and you'll live for an eternity,
as my flower, forever.

Unbroken

Thank you for showing me that I was never broken in the first place.
I was just made to think that I was.

Not used to it

I'm not used to you.

I don't know how to feel,
to have someone really listen to me,
or when you say 'It's okay',
when I tell you that I'm busy.

Why aren't you mad?
When I hang around beautiful girls,
or leave you on *Read*,
there was no whirlwind you unfurled.

You said you'd love me still,
even when I don't foot the bill,
and you hugged me tighter,
when my world was in disorder.

Simply put,
when we're together,
you loved me completely and unselfishly,
like no one, has ever.

They'll see you

The world will realize how amazing you are,
through me.

Immortalized,
parts of you live in me for eternity.

You reflect me

We're quite alike,
you and I.

By loving you wholeheartedly,
I've learned how to love me.

You can still love another,
while fighting an inner war,
there's still beauty in seeing in color,
even if it's a mix of rainbows and gore.

Growing old

I've dreamt of a heaven where it's just us two. We'd wake up before the sun rises because our cats said so, and we'd take a walk by the beach and watch the sun carefully paint our world.

You'd complain about your joints and your deteriorating eyesight, and I'd joke about it, making you smile. My crow's feet are proof of how much you've made me laugh over the years, and your smile lines would tell me that I've done the same for you. We'd hold hands and walk up to the bakery to see the baker's children off to school, and I'd buy you a pink carnation for your hair just to make you feel beautiful. I want to love you like this for the rest of the time I have left, for you have so graciously created this heaven for me, without my request.

Recall

When I feel like there will be *no more love in my future*,
all I have to do is recall the very moment
I said those words years ago,
and how life eventually gave me,
you.

Love you too

I'll love you from your head to your toes,
and protect you from everything you hate.

For you, I'll eat your peanuts and tomatoes,
and take you on our favorite dates.

Never see your kindness as a crutch,
for it is why I'm deeply attracted to you.

If I could love you all that much,
maybe, you could try to love you too.

Favorite memory

I asked you what your favorite memory was,
and with stars in your eyes,
you recounted a perfect day without me in it.

I took it personally.

So, I made it a challenge to give you my best,
and until you change your answer,
I will not rest.

Words felt

Our silence is nothing short of emptiness,
or so I've heard,
instead, it is filled with magic,
that never found its home in words.

Your eyes say everything,
although nothing is said at all,
these are beautiful moments,
that give memories a little more.

The stillness fill our ears,
with poetry our eyes recite,
stuck in a breakable silence,
no one wants to defy.

We waited patiently
but only quietness was dealt,
it's fine though,
for words unsaid,
were most often,
words felt.

With half of your heart

With half of your heart,
my blood pumps quicker than before.
Time no longer has an end or start,
as we lie here, on my bedroom floor.

With half of your heart,
my heart has found its rhythm.
Emotions to calm or to quicken,
it can't differentiate them.

With half of your heart,
what should feel heavier,
instead, now feels lighter.
Our burdens are now shared,
fairly with one another.

With half of your heart,
I filled the empty crevice,
with can bes and will bes,
with half of your heart.

whole

We both had enough broken pieces,
to build ourselves a whole new person.

Xmas lights

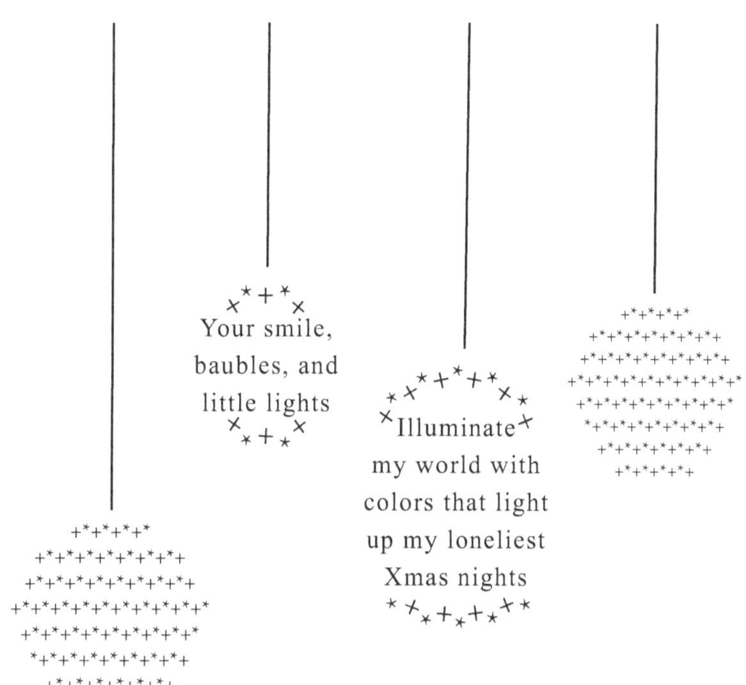
Your smile,
baubles, and
little lights

Illuminate
my world with
colors that light
up my loneliest
Xmas nights

Blind faith

Blind faith is credulous,
based on feelings with a past,
but our love needs no evidence,
for love is blind and so is its path.

The Allegory of the Sun

One must first recognize the sunset before looking into the sun,
as I've embraced its darker side before knowing that you were the one.

Undeserving

"I'm undeserving of happiness,
my flaws taint your perfection.

Close your heart,
it's your only protection,
for I don't deserve you,
and your affection."

-

"That's odd, I feel like I don't deserve you either.
Do two negatives make it a positive, I wonder?"

I live for you

Because of you,
I want to live.

I'm glad,
that our dreams of love,
are no longer make-believe.

I'm leaving all my baggage behind,
heart light, cares cast into the wind,
and with your little hand held tight in mine,
we'll travel far into cloud nine,
dressed to the nines with wine.

Our story

There might be numerous chapters of fast-paced drama
wedged between beautiful calms,
but I know we will be more than okay with the ending,
when it comes.

A love bond

Never would I do you the injustice,
of just feeling in love with you.

Our souls would be in an inseverable bond,
transcending all fickleness, that is *feelings*.

Our destiny will have been etched in fate far beyond,
further than any conscious understanding.

Our love bond is never dead.
It breathes and grows with us.
for we would have only scratched the surface,
of how we'd pull through all seven-year itches.

Feelings fleet far, but bonds bind.
Love me, my dearest,
and I'll promise you in kind.

The captive

I twirled, slid, and jumped like a fool,
across the icy wasteland you call a heart.
Enamored, you think I'm beautiful,
gliding effortlessly, while looking the part.

Oh, how the icy winds pierced my skin,
they heckled an impossible win.
but I made you fall for my routine,
and then, quite soon with me.

Your eyes followed me while
my blades slid over your skin,
creating beautiful mandalas,
drawing you from within.

Soon, the music chimed for a final move,
it was a triple axel,
right above the thinnest part of you.

You shattered, but I held you together,
captives no more, we are now free,
forever.

Little one

Open your eyes, little one,
to an adventure we enjoy only once.

Open your fingers, one by one,
feel it all and find it all, go on a hunt.

Free your mind, little one,
knowledge is infinite, you are never done.

Bare your heart, little one,
and love those who think they have none.

Exhausted for you

I know what it takes to be a good partner,
and it's exhausting.
The emotions, risks, and identity you lose,
think about the effort, time and money too.

It's exhausting to be amazing at loving you.

"You'll have more energy for the ones you love."
You know that never lasts,
and soon you'll be praying to the ones above.

I want to be amazing for you.
Or not at all.

It's not easy reigniting a fire, we believe,
especially if the other doesn't know how.
People change; you either adapt or leave,
the latter being the popular one now.

Do I find myself smiling with you at the end of an exhausting day?
Well if it is, I'm ready to be exhausted for you, every day.

I'm glad

I'm glad we ended.

I'm glad we stopped pretending to love each other.
But it wasn't time wasted,
for it taught us how to love our future others.

Adrenaline Shots

Self love-tred

You can't love yourself without knowing
which parts you hate.
You can't accept yourself without knowing
which imperfections you have to accept.

Harmonies

Why live your life in harmony,
when you can be the main melody?

The nature of Love

Love is difficult to understand,
yet, so simple to know.

Love is many things.

Love is an emotion.
Love lives in affection, sacrifice,
devotion, selflessness, passion,
respect, and loyalty.

Love is a connection.
Love is romantic, patriotic, biochemical,
egotistical, familial, theological,
materialistic, or friendly.

Love exists in all of them,
or sometimes, within none at all.

I thank love for all of its facets,
and centuries of illogical mysteries,
love can belong to all who breathe,
but it can also solely belong to me.

Weakness/Strength

Not all weaknesses need to be fixed,
not all strengths need to be exploited.

Weaknesses turn into strengths at times,
and strengths only exist,
when weaknesses are recognized.

No pain, no gain.

Plunge deep, harvest, and create from your pain.
If you want beautiful flowers, you need a little rain.

False courage

Do not wait for anger or sadness to be honest,
like alcohol, they do not teach you true courage.

Tongues and Minds

Sharp minds may have blunt tongues,
while sharp tongues possess dull minds.

High intelligence may breed arrogance,
while tactlessness stems from ignorance.

Thin skin

"You're superwoman.
Your skin is so thick you could take on anything."

"I'm this way because of my thin skin. I feel everything.
I hurt the most, and that's how I learn the most."

Her sun

She might be a drop in a sea of people,
but every wave had a fragment of her sun.

Learn to break yourself

I encourage you to fall in love.

Get your heart broken too,
and learn how to fix it anew.

If you want to understand,
you need to know what's inside.
Break it with your own hands,
or risk living without true sight.

Be revered

Death is not evil,
it's regret that people fear,
learn and fail at everything,
live a life all will revere.

Passed time

Passed time can never be a measure,
of how genuine a love is.

Measure love by the future years you see yourself loving her,
not by the years you've already did, my dear.

It's Okay.

You don't need to be in a relationship,
to feel socially accepted.
It is known that it is difficult to love yourself.
What more,
if you expect someone else to do it for you?

You don't need to be making millions of dollars,
to feel socially accepted.
Money gives you freedom of choice,
but it doesn't give you freedom of the mind.

You don't need to feel happy all the time,
to feel socially accepted.
Everyone is just as sad as you are,
no matter where they are.

It's okay to throw in the towel,
just make sure you get back in there quickly,
fresh and clean after your shower.

It's okay if you don't have all these things,
to feel self-acceptance.

It's okay to just... be.

And if they do come your way,
treasure it.
And if they leave,
learn from it.

Herd mentality

Have you heard the herd?
Follow!
Or risk being hurt.

Are you a part of the herd?
If you're not,
risk not being heard.

Do you like the herd?
Of course, you do!
Don't be absurd.

Thinking of leaving the herd?
Oh, so what if you're a bird?

-

Other birds flock along,
But I'm more of an eagle,
Lonely but strong.

Peace

You'll never have peace of mind,
if you keep giving them a piece of your mind.

Honesty and trust

Half truths made to protect oneself
are often masked as false nobility for someone else.

Although real truths are sometimes uglier,
their outcomes are usually way prettier.

It takes years of honesty,
to build an ounce of trust.

Hence, you're no longer trustworthy,
if you are no longer worth my trust.

Digital connection

We're lens to lens,
when I'd much prefer it eye to eye.

Emojis mask your true emotions,
invisible tears, and words not spoken.

Tap me on my shoulder and we'll talk,
cause nothing really happens if you just tap-stalk.

We wonder why we feel dejected,
oh how could it be,
that we're more disconnected,
in a hyperconnected society?

142

5000 millisecond rule

You have 5 seconds to pick yourself up again,
when your self-esteem drops.

Do not linger too long in the rain,
for that time could be used,
to climb back to the top.

Differently

Do things differently,
to fail differently.

Others may be indifferent
to your different failures,

but always-
remain focused in deference
until you succeed differently.

Love what you do

I don't know if you knew,
that although you aren't mine,
I've never stopped caring for you.

With blind faith, you told me your future—
to be an astronaut, president or a teacher.

I'll learn with you,
enrich you,
and guide you,
even though at times,
I might not know how to.

Soon enough,
I will not have all the answers.

You will create new chapters,
and be your own master.

One day,
you might teach too,
and hopefully, just like me,
love what you do.

Encourage me

They're not words of encouragement if you need them to feel superior,
like a drug, in a minute you're back to feeling inferior.

Do not depend on others to build your worth,
but be better than who you were yesterday,
and that will be enough.

The chase

When you chase someone,
you change yourself.

They fall for the mirage you can never outrun,
and the unrealistic expectations of the self.

Work hard and become the person you want,
let it flow, for all love stories are their own.

Show your truest self to the one,
and if they want you, you will know.

Lightning

You may think you've stolen my thunder,
but what the lightning strikes is what matters.

You'll never know

Hardships and problems are just like spies,
they're just hidden blessings in disguise.

Don't just bloom

"Bloom where you're planted," he says,
ignoring the true meaning of the phrase.

I'm not just a pretty little flower,
a harmless thing, one freely takes.

Instead,
remember me as a flowing river,
leaving a trail of life in my wake.

When will I truly be happy?

You will break, but you will learn,
have some patience, you'll get your turn.

What is my purpose?

Life is the purpose.
Having a purpose is life.

Is having a purpose the meaning of life?
Or is being alive, the purpose?

Can we purposely propose our purpose?
And can a pursued purpose become a pure purpose?

How purposeful can we be?
How alive can we truly feel?

Another way

Maybe in another life, I'll take that road,
but now, I'm ready to go the other way.

Without a doubt that wherever I go,
I know I'll be fine,
I'll be okay.

You are not a flower

You are not a flower waiting to be plucked against your will,
trimmed obediently to look beautiful by the sill,
you're not a part of the service of bees who only come and go,
beautiful for only a season, a limited-time show.

But be soil and rock,
unseen, trodden but strong.
Elevate civilizations, plot transformation,
even if history gets your name wrong.

Be water,
take any form, move slow and fast,
carve continents while giving life to the softest blade of grass.

It's a pity, if you think life is just all about being pretty,
Just know that,
pretty things get pretty boring, pretty quickly.

Home wrecker

A woman of principle will only bring the truth of your disloyalty
to her fellow woman of principle.
Do not underestimate the unspoken bond between these women
thinking that you, sir, are invincible.

Be strong

You're given a gift of strength,
so use it wisely.
Be strong for others to the death,
never take it lightly.

Your protection will not make them weak,
it buys them time to create new techniques.
You might be a mess of broken pieces on the inside,
but hope for their potential future will keep you alive.

My Universe

My universe,
I've loved you,
before I've even met you.

Never did I expect,
that someone so perfect,
could come from someone so far from it.

You'll say that you hate me,
but I'll know you'd never mean it,
you'd say that you didn't ask to be born
into a world that's on the verge of crumbling,
and that it's selfish of me to want to bring you here,
it wasn't your choosing.

Just know that it is my duty,
to show you a life worth living,
for this is a one in a trillion opportunity,
to be a part of this temporary,
but permanent history.

How beautiful it is,
to witness a broken person fall in love with an imperfect world,
with so much ugliness and sadness in and around you,
one day you'll see,
that there's always hope,
and that life,
can be a pretty amazing place to be.

157

Empty shoes

Sometimes, shoes are not meant to be filled.
They're meant to be tossed out to make way for wheels.

Adjusting your lenses

Zoom out and disassociate when your problems get too big,
zoom in and appreciate when you're feeling small.

Two roads

Two roads diverged in a yellow wood,
but I took the one less traveled by.
The journey was tough and I did all I could,
but ended up on the road most traveled by.

Went back to school and listened well,
learned the craft and got out of my shell.
I got much older, became a little bit wiser,
and returned to the woods with a plan and a charter.

And there it was, two roads diverged still,
one beautiful and the other promising thrill.
We chanted once and set foot thither,
very afraid and a little brave together.

We threaded carefully into the thick of it,
and found ourselves further up the split.

Aha!

We're back on the road most traveled by,
cracked a laugh and said our goodbyes.

My 12 rules

1. Be kind, just to be kind.
2. Love, just because.
3. Be grateful, because you can be.
4. Have patience, because time is but a construct.
5. Be honest, although it hurts.
6. Know what respect means to yourself and to others.
7. Be very excited as a beginner.
8. Forgive, for we all have different concepts of what is or is not offensive.
9. Advocate, but with love.
10. Support, not to expect support in return.
11. Listen to understand, not to reply.
12. Self-reflect to understand, not to penalize.

Perspective

'They told me that she was too much, too vicious,
but I told them that she was just ambitious.'

'They said that she didn't have a filter,
but I told them that her honesty is what I love about her.'

Ignite

I want to be close to you,
close enough to feel the burn
you radiate true.

Grant me the fortune to bathe—
in the waves of your energy,
as you set the world ablaze,
with your legacy.

Turn me to dust,
watch the world combust.

Grace us with your light,
don't hold back,
ignite.

What I wish I knew

Do not give yourself to someone who only cares about how you look on their arm. They will buy you clothes to change you and remember your favorite flowers just to use them against you.

Never be with someone who demands gratitude from you. Do not fall in love with the light they bring into your life when all they have been using is a rusty old gaslight.

But bind yourself to the one who buys you books that fuel your dreams and someone who sings off-key with you. Take notice of the person who tapes up that little blinking light on the AC just so that it doesn't bother you while you sleep. Stay with the one who listens to you.

Be with someone who is honest and respectful. They will show you that they love you in private often, not caring if the world sees. Stand by the person who understands their flaws but will not weaponize them.

Devote your heart to the one who treats your pets like their very own children. Radiate with someone who has dreams of their own and is not afraid of chasing them.

And above all, never leave a person who makes you feel at home, when you're in places that no one can ever call it so.

We're all fairies

'I need you to believe in me so that I can continue to exist.'
'You have to believe in you, so that **you** can continue to exist, not me, not him, **you.**'

3 things

I yearn for a soul who completes me spiritually,
and a perfectly imperfect body to love unconditionally.
I crave a mind who challenges me mentally,
by rationalizing, intelligently.

But, if they are only two of these things,
they will not be for me.

Ho'oponopono

It's time to meet your inner child,
for it's a reunion that's long overdue.
Find her being one with the wild;
watch her smile like you used to.

Is she happy or is she sad?
Look deep into her eyes,
and show her that you care.
Envelope her in your arms,
and thank her for always being there.

Tell her that you're sorry,
for neglecting her fears,
and ignoring the many stories,
you said you promised you'll hear.

Ask her for her forgiveness,
for all the wrong that you have done,
end it by telling her that you love her,
and say it all again,
three more times,
one by one.

There's this and that

Less is more,
more or less,
life has its up and downs,
so be down for it,
when you're up.

People come and go,
so go along,
when they come,
let them go,
if they no longer come.

Do's and don'ts don't do,
for not all is black and white,
look for hidden hues,
always question the light.

Authenticity

Authenticity
is felt, not seen.

Oh, the audacity,
for you to come to me,
to give me an opportunity,
I don't even need.

Friendships to you are but a utility,
a tool, for seeking charity,
funny how you disguise it all as philanthropy,
when you're the only beneficiary.

Emoceans

I let my salty tears
fall into the sand
and watch them
get licked away
by the waves.

The sea,
takes my salt
and melds it within itself
selflessly
without looking
into the memories
trapped in each fallen grave.

It shows solidarity
by not having said anything at all,
as it dances and caresses me
in its swirling winds.

The light grants me sight
as I send my hurt
far into its horizons,
taking me further and deeper
to places I've yearned.

Fight or flight?

Where do we go?
What do we do?
Stay put, or go?
We don't know.

Pack your bags,
and your emotions,
know your flag,
and devotions.

Stay low,
go high,
or across the ocean,
run in a zig-zag,
or halt all motion.

Do what you must, carefully,
but think about your society,
and all of humanity.

171

Break the bias

S(he's) passionate, not emotional,
S(he's) empathetic, not a pushover.
S(he's) collected, not mechanical,
S(he's) driven, not a bulldozer.
S(he's) has ideas, not just opinionated,
S(he's) just like you, but discriminated.

Make time

They say time is but a construct,
so why let it take over,
when it is us,
who has the power to construct it?

Forgive yourself

Forgive yourself
for choosing love over security.

Forgive yourself
for not wanting to start a family.

Forgive yourself
for giving up a little too early.

Forgive yourself
for not following the rules of society.

There is no one true way to live a fulfilling and responsible life,
for we have control over what gives us strife.

Forgive yourself.

174

Ratings

Think about who brought out the best and worst in you, not just by how they have treated you. Did they help you to become who you want to be, or stray further away from it? Are you proud of who you have become? Who made you feel your best or your worst? Rate the different versions of your past too, because it's never just them. It's you too.

Try better

Failures take you closer.
Don't just try again,
try better.

Imaginary

Imaginary friends,
keep you company,
while imaginary children,
keep you on your toes.

Imaginary friends,
want you to go crazy,
while imaginary children,
will be afraid if you let go.

We all want to become the
best versions of ourselves,
before bringing the imaginary into reality.

Put the goal of perfection
back on the shelves,
and strive for authenticity.

Your children will love you,
even if they see the cracks,
show them all that you can do,
and humbly admit what you lack.

Just keep swimming

I still struggle to put my head above water,
but you've given me a mask to see,
and taught me how to breathe.

We know the journey might seem like forever,
but I know I'll end up where I'm meant to be.

Bottling them up

Day by day,
I bottle them up,
I put them all on display,
without spilling a drop.

Months go by,
and I soon ran out of space,
bottles blocked the door,
they piled up to the sky,
and took every
inch of the floor.

I can no longer move,
I no longer knew what to do.
Overwhelmed,
blank, and afraid,
I opened them up,
one by one,
and I drank.

I drank 'til I was
full of my feelings.
They spilled, mixed, and
smelled appalling.
It wasn't pretty,
but they were slowly
disappearing.

They tasted bitter; like waste,
but over time, I've learned how to
appreciate the taste.
I used the rest of it
to make paint for the walls,
and ink for poetry.

I also dyed my hair and
dunked my plain white t's,
into tubs filled to the brim
with mixed feelings.

The empty bottles are nothing more than vases
for flowers and worn-out pencils now,
for my feelings are now free to roam and create,
any way they know how.

30

The big three-oh is a milestone,
that comes with anxiety, formed by society.
"Watch your body clock,"
Tick-tock, tick-tock.

But not you.

You define time,
happiness, loneliness,
love, and satisfaction.

Make mistakes, choose your strives,
for there's not one way to live a life.
There's no ladder to climb, or final destination,
to reach in time.

Appreciate the mornings,
close your eyes, and smell the rain.
For life cannot be life,
without a little pain.

What you deserve

Pitiful soul,
you deserve the good in life.
You **deserve** the good in life.

Lonely child,
you deserve a gentle love that cares,
and to thrive as a circle in a world of squares.

Oh, beautiful neglected spirit,
if you only knew how wonderful
you are when you let your heart see it.
"I feel guilty, the moment I feel joy",
Stop.
for only you have the power to destroy,
to love, forgive and **be okay.**

Note to little self

1. Love unselfishly and see the best in people who need it most for they are unable to do it on their own.

2. Be content. Striving for something as temporary as happiness will ensure your demise.

3. Want little. Have little. Worry little.

4. Figure out how everything works. Some of it will prove useful someday. Heck, it might even save your life.

5. Heartbreaks will do more good than harm to you.

6. Have integrity and respect. Never do something you don't want to happen to you.

7. Unlearn and relearn how you love.

Crush it

Crush every little crush,
and smother every single butterfly.

Rush to numb the rush,
and archive all their replies.

Sorry to be blunt,
but you're just bored, my dear,
give yourself two whole months,
and I promise, the disease will clear.

My medicine

Prepare two affirmations.
Take one in the morning,
and one in the evening before you go to bed.

And when feeling burned out and exhausted,
take a chill pill and rest your head.

When proven wrong,
take a bitter pill after having a slice of humble pie.
It's a hard pill to swallow, so do it carefully.

Taste your own medicine,
before giving it away; don't lie.
I've learned it the hard way, regretfully.

And when in doubt, laugh it off and pay no attention to faults,
because at times,
a little humor can be the best medicine of all.

A new dawn

An unwinnable battle has been won,
with all past faults forgiven and foregone.

Here's a salute to the hearts who pressed on,
rise in faith, for a hope of a new dawn.

Psychedelics

Mssing Pices

It may seem crzy,
bt I fnd new resons to lve yu,
evn whn yu're nt hre wth me.

Evry sngle day,
I mss the pices tht I hve gven to yu;
pices tht ar nw lost,
far, far awy.

Hidden message

Hurry along,
It's time to go my dear,
I promise I won't cry, not a ingle tear.
I'm a big girl, you've got nothing to fear,

Go on,
Isn't that your axi I hear?
Your impossible drems are long overdue,
Craz adventures await, they beckon for you.

s-t-a-y

A lvoe Peom

Yuor smlie, dsioirenitnig,
yuor sgianls, cnoufinsig,
yuor wrods, bfafling,
ftuure palns, unwknoiwng
but, teh mroe I lvoe you,
the cleraer it gets and,
only tmie will tell,
when I'll undrestnad,
why you and I,
make absolute sense.

Messed up

My world was əpısdn uʍop
My ʇɹɐəɥ , the wrong side up.

Then you came, turned me dnuora,

Loved me; my world you've warped .

It's not like it's any better than before,
But it's a kind of different,

I adore.

Hurt when hurt

H umans
U nderestimate
R eal
T rust
W alls
H ide
E very
N aked

H abit,
U rge,
R egret,
T ediously.

Poof!

o   d   ear   w   h   en,
O' dear, when?

A

Amazing actors artificial Alphas are,
always angry and always asking.

Artificial Alphas also avoid actual action,
after asserting abominable authority.

Affected allies are always alarmed and abused,
absorbing agony and antidepressants.

Artificial Alphas are anathemas.

B

Be better before betraying,
before blaming,
before bullying,
before boasting,
before bantering.

Believe balanced beliefs before being,
because beliefs beget behavior.

C

Current community challenges:

- Conservative caregivers cultivate complacent characters,
- Controlling civilizations create complex, compulsive consequences.
- Cyber criminals camouflage comfortably,
- Casted champions compete convincingly.

D

Dream, darling; dream,
direct discipline,
don't doubt,
don't delay,
dive deep,
Do.

Declare daily.

E

Every evil embodies earthly egos,
empathy enlightens, educates; extends experience even.

F

1. Fake friends formulate flattery for future favors, familiar, faithful friends flatten facades.

2. Fearing failure formulates foolish feelings, for fear forsakes fine, foreseeable futures.

G

Giving genuine gratitude,
garners gradual growth; generates glee.

H

He helped her hack happiness.
Her heart had hope.

Her husband heard.

Her husband hit her; hunted him.
Her hands hasped, hoping.

He hurried, he hid.

Her husband hears him; hacks him.

Her heart howls.
Her husband hacked her happiness.

I

I'm indecisive if I internalize,
I'm inflexible if I idealize.

I impersonate if I'm insecure,
I..I'm insecure if I impersonate.

Imagination induces illogical illusions,
logical illusions inspire impact.

J

Justice judges judgemental, jealous jerks.
Journalists joke, jesters jeer,
justifications jinxed, jaws jitter.

K

Kindhearted knowledgeables kill know-it-alls.
Karma knows kindness.

L

Loyal love lasts; learns laboriously & liberates logic.
Loyal love lasts; learns laboriously & liberates.
Loyal love lasts; learns.
Loyal love lasts.
Love lasts.
Love.

M

My mind misses...
my mother's moments.

Mixed moods,
missed meals,
mourning mornings,
missing motivations–

Maybe, mother misses me more.

N

Nature needs nicer neighbors, now.
Neglected,
nature negotiates numerous, necessary nightmares.

O

Opposites attract, but they also oblige.
Observe occurring oppression of opinions,
outgrow outdated oaths.

P

Poetry personifies people's philosophy,
provides personal, perfect places.

Poetry pardons pain,
paralyzes prejudice,
promises peace.

Q

Qualified questioners quote quality questions,
quivering quitters quarrel quickly.

R

Remember, reading rears rhetorical reasoning,
repels resentful rationales respectfully,
rekindles reverence regarding rough realities.

S

She smiled sweetly,
supported simply.

She showed surfaced satisfaction,
still, she suffered silently.

Separation suggested,
sentiments suspended,
Souls severed.

She slipped.

Should've said sorry sooner,
should've seen signs.

T

Take thy troubles to transformed thinkers,
those tempting, twisted thoughts that tear time.
Thank these thinkers; they turn terrors to teachings.

These thoughts that trigger tears today,
throw them toward tall tides tomorrow.

Try these traditions together, to thrive.

U

Unfortunate uncertainties unite us until urgent ultimatums urge understanding. Unknowingly, unconvinced underdogs undo unity.

V

Very vocal victims vanish vainly,
valuable vendetta videos veiled.

Voices vacuumed, votes voided,
Voila! Vindicated victory visualized.

W

We wonder why we're weak,
when we willingly woo worry.

X

X Xenophobia,
XoXo Xenophilia.

Y

Yield yearning your yesteryears.
You're young,
yet you yearn yesterday's youth?

Z

Zealous zest zaps zillions.
Zombified zeroes ziplock.

Sleeping pills

Quarantined

Okay, journalling. What do I even say...?

How do people even journal? Am I supposed to start with a 'Dear Diary'? This feels like an activity for a twenty-something-year-old girl going through an identity crisis. My wife has been quite encouraging though, she says that I could learn a lot about myself if I put my thoughts down on paper. I guess I'll do this once a week.

Alright... So uh...

Journal entry #1
Date: August 24th, 2025.
Time: 6.34 pm

Dear journal, how are you doing?
Dear journal? This is so stupid.

I guess I should introduce myself although you're clearly an inanimate object. My name's Marcus. Marcus Ting. Yeah, like the *Some Ting Wrong* - kinda *Ting*. My colleagues get quite a bit of a laugh out of that. The whole reason why I'm talking to you today, or lack for the better word, *writing* to you today, is for me to *express my feelings and thoughts in a healthy way.* I wasn't sure why gaming all day and cooking dinner for your wife every night was deemed unhealthy for my mental health, but I guess I'll give it a shot.

Life has been pretty okay I guess, I wake up, take a shower, have breakfast with Cassidy, and—

Oh, my bad. Allow me introduce you to my beautiful, perfect wife. She has the longest, thickest black hair and the cutest button nose. Her body is to die for, she does perfect impersonations of the late Jenna Tvrovinsky and paints the most thought provoking paintings. She's every man's fantasy wife. I still have no idea why she chose to end up with a specky, scrawny geek who codes in the dark for a living.

Cassidy and I married in February 2020, the year the outbreak happened. We were pretty lucky too. We managed to get everyone together for a nice little wedding in Bali, Indonesia before The Quarantine happened. It was absolutely magical. Cassidy really wanted to have a view of the horizon at Uluwatu while we said our vows. And like the award-winning husband that I am, I granted her wish. Thinking about D-day always brings tears to my eyes. I've never seen her so happy, and so beautiful. I think about the days before The Quarantine a lot and we've been hoping for things to go back to the way they were for about five years now, but things are still the same. Bummer.

I hope she doesn't read this, her head would get too big if she knew I called her beautiful twice in my first journal entry. Anyway, that's about it for today. Gotta start on dinner or Mrs. Ting's gonna be hangry. Ha-ha!

Whoa, that's a pretty long first entry. I guess I did have a lot to get off my chest. Plus, I needed to start this strong, Cassidy's looking at me from across the room, making sure that I'm doing this right. Geez, what a micromanager. Ha-ha!

Journal entry #2
Date: August 25th, 2025 (The Next Day)
Time: 9 am

Hey, journal!
I know I've made a commitment to write to you only once a week, but boy, do I have some good news for you! I found baby magazines in Cassidy's makeup drawer! Do you think she's pregnant? I've always wanted a child and she has always been pretty adamant about not being a mom too early in our marriage. She reminded me constantly about how we should *enjoy our marriage* before introducing another member who could potentially dilute our love and attention for each other. Ha-ha!

This is so exciting. Should I confront her? Or should I wait?

Hold on, who am I kidding? You're a book. You're not going to say anything.

Journal entry #3
Date: August 28th, 2025
Time: 12.30 pm

Now that we're officially friends, I'll skip the formalities. It has been three days since I've found the baby magazines and Cassidy still hasn't said a word. She has been acting rather strange lately. For breakfast, she didn't ask for coffee as she used to and she was less chatty. Shouldn't I know what's up?

Alright, got to go. The delivery man is here with our groceries as always, at 12.45 pm. Time to cook us a good lunch!

Journal entry #4
Date: August 28th, 2025 (The Same Day)
Time: 9.45 pm

I'm over the moon! Cassidy noticed how fidgety I was, so she decided to own up and tell me that she is pregnant. She found out a week ago but she wanted to be sure before telling me. I kissed her so hard and made sure to hug her only a little. You know, in case I squashed little me. Or little her. I'm just so excited!

I was THIS CLOSE to calling EVERYONE I know but Cassidy told me that we should wait for at least three months to make sure she completed her first trimester. Makes sense.

I love her even more now.

Journal entry #6
Date: September 5th, 2025
Time: 8.10pm

Wow, being pregnant really changes a person. Luckily for me, Cassidy is becoming more and more beautiful by the day. Her cravings are odd though. She requested that I bake her a chocolate cake with dried chilis in the center. I couldn't stomach it but she absolutely loved it. She scooped up every single crumb... and chili seed too. I'll probably never understand the inner workings of a pregnant lady's ever-changing body.

We had orange juice on the balcony today for tea. We usually have cold chocolate milk and biscuits but Cassidy really wanted something sour to balance out the sweet and spicy chocolate cake she had for lunch. It was wonderful. She told me how excited she was to be a mother and we planned all sorts of vacations we could bring Peanut to. Yes, we named the kid Peanut because we couldn't settle on a name yet. We discussed giving Peanut a unisex name like Alex or Sam. The kid would eventually figure out who they wanted to be in the future and I think that would give Peanut enough freedom to choose.

Alright, I've got to go, Cassidy's calling. Probably another odd craving for fries topped with chocolate syrup?

Journal entry #7
Date: October 23rd, 2025
Time: 3.15pm

Hey Journal,
Apologies for neglecting you. I guess I am not that good at journaling after all. It's really hard to keep up the discipline every week when you're a full-time husband a.k.a. butler to a pregnant wife. I know it's an excuse, but I'm just having the absolute time of my life. Cassidy has been... extra *hot* lately. Not as the hot like smokin' like she always is, but *passionate*. We've been at it all day, all week, and twice the frequency compared to how we were on our honeymoon!

I mean, I'm not complaining but it's starting to get a little bit exhausting. I don't think I can keep up. Plus, wouldn't it damage Peanut? I tried my best to be gentle, but it feels like she's using me to help dig Peanut out of her. On other news, The Quarantine has been extended again for another 3 months and I don't really understand why they keep doing this? It has been five years already and I'm sure everyone is pretty fed up with living cooped up in their homes.

I guess I should talk to you a little bit about The Quarantine. It would be a nice change of topic, one that didn't revolve around my wife. Am I boring you, journal?

Journal entry #8
Date: October 31st, 2025
Time: 9 pm

Okay, I'm back. I'm thinking that I should probably set up a predictable time every week to help with my consistency. Is 9 pm every Friday alright for you?

It's Halloween today. Not that anyone celebrates it nowadays, or any festival for that matter, but we like to remember that certain days meant something to people pre-Quarantine days. Oh yes, I promised you a story on The Quarantine. You were probably still a tree then, you wouldn't have known. Ha-ha!

So, right after Cassidy and I got married in Bali and had our honeymoon, (stay with me here, I'm not segueing) we came home to an empty US airport. The streets were empty, malls were quiet, parks were abandoned- you get the picture. We must've been pouring every bit of attention into each other for those two weeks because we hadn't had the slightest clue or understood the gravity of the situation until we reached home.

Sure, we knew that there was a virus outbreak that was sweeping the globe, but we didn't know that it would reach us so quickly. Everyone was instructed to put themselves under house arrest until the government developed a vaccine. We all had hopes that it would all be over in a year at least, but a mutated version of the virus got accidentally released into the world, plunging the world into further darkness and uncertainty.

The mutated virus was a failed vaccine experiment from a small, independent lab in the suburbs. No one knows. But of course, it came with a variety of quite entertaining conspiracy theories. This demoralized us even further, and stricter lockdowns were implemented across the world at a more rapid rate. It was pretty okay at first, and people adapted to the new living arrangements. Some even testified that it increased their quality of life and productivity. But, five years have passed and we've seen its long term effects on people. Suicide rates were going up, mental health declined exponentially and jobs were stripped away from people. It's really quite dystopian.

I half expected this way of life to happen to one or two generations after me, but little did I know, the virus would bring the future to us now.

Cassidy and I have not left our apartment in five years.

I guess that's enough for today, writing about The Quarantine depresses me. How about we get back to the obsessive wife entries?

Journal entry #9
Date: November 7th, 2025
Time: 9 pm

Journal! I'm back, same time on Friday! Setting a consistent time really helps. Cassidy is so proud of me. I hope you didn't mind me showing her my previous entry about The Quarantine. She was really surprised about how *articulate* and *eloquent* I was. I loved it when she used fancy words on me. Maybe, I should publish them once The Quarantine is over? Ah, another dream set after The Quarantine. When will it ever end?

Cassidy has been experiencing discomfort with Peanut. Should it happen so early in the trimester? It's probably just hormones. We got our home ultrasound machine fired up with our local doctor on video and he assured us that it was nothing to worry about.

Come on, Peanut! Just one more month and you'll be a legitimate fetus!

Journal entry #10
Date: November 15th, 2025
Time: 8 pm

Oops, I'm late by a day. But it doesn't matter, I'm here now.

Cassidy has been pretty down lately. Her *passion* and appetite is dwindled, and she doesn't really talk to me much. She has been cooped up in her room a lot because of the stomach pains she's been getting the past week. She's really, really worried and it's making me worry even more. We've already learned to love Peanut and I think that just makes things more complicated.

Our doctor delivered a hCG test stick this morning. That only made her cry.

Journal entry #11
Date: November 18th, 2025
Time: 11.14 pm

Cassidy didn't have the courage to use the hCG stick until today. She was so brave. The stick told us that Peanut is fine and it perked our spirits right back up. She was still having abdominal pains but we were both trying to remain positive, just like the test. It was Cassidy and I against the world!

I wanted to lighten the atmosphere in the house today, so I set up a vegetarian candlelit dinner for both of us. We talked to Peanut and urged him to stay strong for all of us. We were already a family after all. I wanted us to be a family so badly. It was the only good thing that could have happened during The Quarantine. Peanut was the only thing that gave us a proper reason to live.

Not sure why I'm writing as if Peanut was gone, is it a coping mechanism?

Journal entry #12
Date: November 19th, 2025
Time: 3.43 am

Journal,

I don't know what else to do. Cassidy bled so much.

She woke up at 2 am for a pee (as usual) but I was startled awake by her wailing. I rushed over to the bathroom only to witness my worst nightmare. It was pure horror. There was a pool of blood around her legs and she was sitting on the floor crying. My heart broke into a million pieces. Peanut gave up. Peanut gave up on us.

The paramedics wheeled her into the hospital van and she was driven to the emergency room because she lost a lot of blood. I held her hand the whole way. Her lips were white and she was drifting in and out of consciousness. I was so scared. I couldn't lose her too. Cassidy is my world.

I'm now writing to you outside of the emergency room where Cassidy is being treated. You were the first thing I grabbed before hopping into the van. You are my only friend.

***

"Marc, reread the last journal entry for me, please," requested a strange man in a white lab coat.

"I... can't." I said, averting his eyes.

"Yes, you can Marc. Read it and verbalize the situation on that final entry."

I paused, finding a way to form the emotions into a proper sentence.

"Cassidy... was in the emergency ward. She lost a lot of blood from losing Peanut," I answered, as I felt tears well up in my eyes.

"What does the next entry say?" asked the man.

I turned the page reluctantly and read out the contents. It wasn't hard. It was only three words.

"Cassidy... left us." I choked.

"How do you feel right now, Marc?" asked the man with feigned concern.

"I feel... sad. And angry. And alone," I replied, in between sobs. The man held out a hand gently, suggesting that I place the journal back in his hands.

"Okay Marc, do you remember when this happened?"

More questions. This is torture.

"It happened two years ago. In 2025."

"Great, do you know what year it is right now?" prompted the doctor.

I hesitated, unsure. I squinted at the date on the calendar behind him and tried to form the words. It felt like lead.

"2027... the calendar might be wrong... I-" I stammered.

"When did you write entry #11?" the doctor fired back.

Doubt started to grow in my mind.

"Yesterday," I responded. I only had the energy to give one-worded answers now. Did I write this yesterday?

The ink was still fresh, I had stains on my palms mixed with tears and ink that bled from the entry. I don't understand.

My head was hurting. I closed my eyes.

"Marc? Marc, are you still there?" a voice called out to me, but I couldn't answer.

"Patient #243 had 5 minutes 12 seconds of acute awareness of the present, 2 minutes of increased duration from previous analysis, patient to resume journal therapy," I heard the man mutter a report into his tiny handheld recorder. His voice sounded like a faraway echo. I wonder who was he referring to? I ran my fingers through my hair and tugged hard. The pain in my head was unbearable.

After minutes that felt like hours, the pain in my head melted away. There were a few minutes of silence between me and the man. It looked like he was waiting for a reply.

Why am I here?

Who is he?

I checked my digital watch and it said at 6.45 pm. Time for dinner.

"I'm a friend of Cassidy's. Is there anything else you need from me, Marc? You zoned out for a second." Explained the man.

"I've got to go. Cassidy's waiting at home for me," I shot the words at the man I did not recognize. I wasn't really sure why I was so angry at this man or why I had tears in my eyes.

"Don't forget your journal. Once a week. Cassidy will be helping me monitor you," the man reminded, as he handed me a leather-bound book. I forced out a thank you and headed straight out the door to a car that was waiting for me.

Ah, the things I'd do for my wife.

Journalling. What do I even say...? Sounds like an activity a twenty-something-year-old girl would do.

Cupid's Arrow

Like every other teen romantic comedy, my story starts off with a phone alarm being ignored by a sleep-deprived male teenager; me. I've set the alarm to go off every 10 minutes from 8 am but my hands have learned how to involuntarily shut it off at every interval.

Before you judge me, I set up this cadence the night before when I was extremely determined to go for a healthy morning run after watching a video online teaching me how to combat depression induced by severe heartbreak. I've read up on a couple of journals on how to kick-start a habit, but none of them talked about the extreme dread and the constant debate you put yourself through in the morning.

I reluctantly pulled myself out of bed after the fourth or fifth alarm and got myself ready before 9 am. My dark hair is growing out uncontrollably, and stubble that put me in between hawker food uncle and hobo chic.

Will it be too sunny now?

Oh wait, was that another excuse? Self-aware, I rebuked myself, hurried over to my desk, and packed my pair of wireless earphones and my mobile. My sneakers were brand new. They were a gift from my ex-girlfriend, Jenna. Gosh, even thinking about her name drives me nuts! I think about her every day, and it's excruciating. To think that it has been three months since the break up and I still have not got my life back.

The cool breeze in Subang Jaya park seems to be leaving now that it's getting pretty late in the morning. The park was filled with families with strollers and dogs walking their walkers. It was beautiful, I couldn't remember the last time I've stepped into the park this early. It's so lively and colorful. The huge, leafy trees sheltered the old folks while they did their tai chi, while the smaller trees acted like goalposts for the younger children. I wasn't too embarrassed about my fitness. I played badminton in high school. Casually. Cardio has always been my worst enemy, so I made sure to do a couple of stretches before getting into a slow jog around the park. The pathway wasn't paved well, so it added an extra challenge for me in terms of balance.

With music blaring in my ears and the running app fired up on my mobile, I increased my speed when the pacer told me to. Memories of Jenna flooded in when Spotify decided to mock me by recommending a playlist I put together for her when we started dating. I didn't skip it. I relished the pain that came with it. Am I a masochist?

It was the afternoon of May 2016 when I first laid eyes on her. I briefly remembered a sharp pain in my heart when I looked into her eyes. She told me that she felt it too.

"Maybe it was Cupid?" she laughed.

"Maybe it was." I agreed. Little did I know that a spell like that would ruin me two years later.

I completed a few more rounds around the park, bringing my total distance ran to 3.5 kilometers and decided to call it a day. There was a message on my phone from Joshua, my best friend. If life cast both of us in a movie, he'd be the main character. He was a triathlon athlete at 19, top in his class in college, a regional master debater (this joke was overdone), and a foster parent for abandoned dogs. I look up to him. Joshua told me that he was already at a mamak nearby, having his breakfast. He had an early 20-kilometer bike ride that morning with his other triathlete friends. He told me that Tony, my second best friend, was there too.

Tony is a whole different guy. If life would cast him in a movie, he would be the comic relief. Apparently, he had been at the mamak since 7 am. He went drinking the night before and decided to sober up for three hours. Thinking about it, I wonder how we stayed friends all these years. We're all so different. I may very much be the controlled variable in this very odd science experiment, as I'm not extraordinary or completely hopeless either. A supporting character perhaps.

"Yo, Andy! Over here!"

I could hear Tony's voice from a distance. He's always so loud. I acknowledged him with a nod and let the server know that I had friends waiting for me. The server didn't care.

"Hey, man. How are you doing? Started running, I see," Tony smirked.

"Aren't you pretty lively for a drunk?" I retorted. Joshua smiled with amusement while sipping his too-bubbly teh tarik.

"But yeah, I've started running. Completed 3.5 kilometers around the park. Took me 30 minutes but I'm pretty happy with the pace." I updated Joshua although he never asked.

"Keep it up and you'll be joining me and my running squad for a 21k soon," Joshua encouraged, while Tony groaned in disagreement. The server came and I ordered myself Roti Canai, fried chicken, and teh tarik.

"You look beat. When's the last time you had a haircut, man?"

"Since when have you become my mom, Tony?" I laughed.

"He's right, you know. Go out. See some people. Flirt a little," Joshua laughed.

"I think the accurate phrase was LIVE a little," I corrected.

My food arrived three minutes after I ordered, doubting that it may be someone else's order they no longer wanted. The service here is insane. I tore into my roti canai and described my sad, heartbroken situation. They nodded and laughed at all the right places. I told them about how Jenna was really into Greek mythology and how she suggested that we should break up because another Cupid's arrow had struck her. I laughed at her metaphor at the time. But I wasn't laughing now. I was still stuck, and I didn't know what to do about it no matter how hard I tried.

"How do you remove a Cupid's Arrow?" I asked.

"Don't try to rip it out yourself or let anyone close enough to do it. It won't end well for you." Joshua said as a matter of factly.

"Then, what should I do?" I asked, while Tony slowly drifted into his own thoughts.

"You could shave down the ends of the arrow, but a little bit of it is going to stay in your heart forever. This way, your heart looks good on the outside and you won't bleed. It'll hurt you every day though." Joshua continued.

"Or, you could numb your heart. It won't look too pretty but at least it won't hurt anymore. But you have to numb it forever for it to work. I use alcohol to do it." Tony added. I've never expected Tony to be involved in this sort of conversation.

"Guys, it's hopeless. There's no way." I sighed.

"Oh, I know! You could chop the arrowhead off and start by pulling it out slowly. Once it's out, you need to hold your heart as tight as you can until the bleeding and crying stops. It'll hurt a lot at first, and it takes FOREVER, but that's the only way your heart can be ready for Cupid again," a small, light voice from behind me interjects.

I turned my body to face the mysterious interjector only to find out that she was the most beautiful girl I've ever seen. Her round eyes were ebony black, and she had straight hair that reached her shoulders. *Please be my age, and single, please be my age and single,* I chanted. Both my friends froze and waited patiently for my blunder.

"Hi, I'm Andy. Thanks for that. It was a really interesting insight," I said while reaching out my hand for a handshake.

"What's he doing? Giving feedback for a presentation?" I hear Tony whispering loudly to Joshua. Joshua laughed in reply. She accepted my handshake and introduced herself as Diana. She had brown skin that seemed to glow under these cheap fluorescent mamak lights. A few moments after, I felt an incoming sharp pain in my heart. But it quickly melted away when her boyfriend returned from the washroom. My friends relished in my misery. I scoffed in defeat and continued tearing into my meal while shifting the subject to Tony's recent drunken tales.

I guess this journey of getting over Jenna is probably going to take a lifetime. Maybe fate will bring us together again, or maybe it won't. Diana's right. It shouldn't stop me from living and doing whatever I can to love again. I deserve to be loved by the right person, and moping around missing her isn't going to bring her back. When the right one comes, I'll know it for sure, and we will love each other in the purest sense of the word. I know it. It will get better.

I will get better.

Not the main character

"Alright, that's the last of it, miss..."

"Bridget.. Bridget Walters. I offer me thanks." The young village girl's admiration for Arthur bled through her eyelashes, too obvious and appalling to ignore. Arthur heaped the last of Bridget's market groceries into her carriage and rewarded her with a wink. Toying with her little flower braid, she watched Arthur as he walked away from her carriage, focusing on what may seem, his well-formed derrière.

Ah. Arthur, always the hero, the charming, handsome one.

Right about now, you'd wish you had access to Arthur's inner monologues. But you're in my head instead. Unfortunately.

I'm Bernard, Arthur's loyal sidekick and best friend. Often funny, occasionally sarcastic, or both. My hair may not be as luscious or thick as his, or jawline as sharp, but we do look a lot like brothers, as so the other villagers say. He has two dimples, and I have one. He has six well-defined abdominals with protruding veins running down his arms, and I have four okay ones, on a good day. Not that I'm keeping count. Sigh, I need a hobby.

"Bernardino, up for a ride? Aurora just had her shoes done and I miss her so." Aurora is Arthur's handsome dark steed, awarded graciously by the village mayor for Arthur's wonderful deeds.

"The number of ways you bastardize my name is astounding. Thank you for keeping my identity somewhat discreet if trouble should ever come my way, brother."

Arthur laughed in reply to my sarcasm. I am often glad to be the one with the personality.

We made our way to the stables and geared up our horses, eager to ride, when a loud bang from one of the houses down south interrupted our brotherly banter.

"What was that? Let's check it out!" exclaimed Arthur in his heroic baritone voice. I echoed, of course. Each gallop increased in speed, guiding our thudding hearts along with it. The closer we got to the noise, the lower my heart sank. We exchanged worried glances as we galloped in the direction of Arthur's home.

Throngs of people surrounded the premises, blocking our path. The roof of his home was completely smashed in and blood was everywhere. Arthur was a man who managed his emotions well, but nothing prepared him for this. He flung himself off Aurora and pushed himself through the crowd to find his mother lying helpless and bloody on the ground. Even though I knew it was already too late, I ordered a boy nearby to call for the village healer to come at once. A few neighbors and I helped move some of the house debris off Gwendolyn. She was bleeding so much.

Arthur's anger was mixed with sorrow, and streams of raging tears raced down his cheeks. His mother beckoned him closer, and he put his ear close to her trembling lips. Arthur's hand pressed tight on her bleeding rib; it was his last desperate attempt to gain a few more moments with her. She used every ounce of energy she had left to whisper her final words. He told her he loved her, nodded, and removed a piece of paper attached to a small trinket from her sleeve. He folded it into his pocket so quickly that no one but I was able to witness it. I was crying too and I felt every single bit of pain Arthur felt.

"Who, or what could have done this?!" eyes frantic, as I shouted the question into the crowd.

No one answered me.

Arthur was orphaned that very day.

We buried Gwendolyn in the old cemetery under the old oak tree where the sun always kissed first. She would be happy there. She always enjoyed its shade during hot summers. Standing shoulder to shoulder by her gravestone, Arthur and I placed a bouquet of lilies and bid his mother farewell one last time, albeit more peacefully. One by one, the villagers leave after paying their final respects.

"I would need to travel to Desolate Mountain. I'm leaving tonight." Rid of all emotion, in a lowered voice he told me his plan without expecting a reply.

"What? That mountain is riddled with wraiths and gypsies! You have no business there," I replied in disbelief. Arthur glanced around our perimeter to make sure we were out of earshot and view. He unfolded the little piece of paper and pressed the trinket firmly into my hand. It felt heavy, but not in the way I thought. It felt like it had a soul. I couldn't recognize the symbols scribbled on the paper too. Nothing made sense.

"These symbols are from an ancient language only spoken by an old tribe north of the Desolate Mountain. The trinket holds a piece of the soul of the angel who protected the human race a millennia ago. My mother was a guardian of this piece, and these items are the key to entering their tribe safely."

"She said that all in one breath?"

Arthur looked at me with contempt.

"No, she didn't. She told me stories of this legend when I was little. But to me, it was nothing but a good story. I never knew that she was preparing me for this mission."

"And what is that exactly? What are you supposed to do when you get there?"

"I don't know," he pondered.

"Vague travel itineraries, murderous tribes, trapped ancient souls with possible danger at every corner- sounds like a fun trip. I'm coming with you," I offered.

In a beat he agreed. I would have at least thought that he would stop me by caring a little bit more for my safety and wellbeing, but I guess as brave as Arthur portrays himself to be, he's afraid too. We shared a few moments of silence.

"I'll supply the horses," I said as I hurried off back to town, leaving Arthur some time alone to grieve.

***

"It should take us about two days to reach the foot of Desolate Mountain," Arthur exclaimed up ahead. The path was too narrow and rough to have us ride side by side. The trees thinned and died out the further we traveled away from the village, acting like a clear message to turn back.

"Yeah, praying that nothing comes out to eat us," I whispered under my breath.

"I heard you. Anyway, it's getting dark, let's set up camp here. I'll take first watch."

Typical Arthur, always barking orders. Being too exhausted to retort, I agreed by halting my horse near our campsite. We'd been riding for what felt like hours, and we really needed the rest if we were to excel on this arduous, uncertain journey.

We broke some bread, had an apple each, and set up a small fire to keep warm. Arthur twirled the trinket in between his fingers while trying to decipher the symbols.

"You can't really read that, can you?" I doubted while tearing a piece of bread between my teeth.

"They feel⋯ familiar. I just can't put my finger on it."

"Do you think whatever came for your mother, might come for us too?"

His eyes darkened at my statement, and shoved the item back into his pocket.

"Let's hope not. And if they do, we'll be ready for them," he said while positioning his bow and arrow right in front of him. Sleep claimed me quite quickly after that.

***

I woke up to the sound of hushed whispers. It was from two people, Arthur and a woman.

"HAIL MARIA! ARTHUR!" I staggered up to get myself ready to act when Arthur cautioned me to stand down. She held a small knife inches from Arthur's throat, and he had his hands restrained. He was propped up against a boulder against his will, but continued to hold an intense glare at the woman. I couldn't move. I was tied up too and was lying flat on my stomach.

"Kerika root. A natural sleeping drug when administered via the neck vein. Clever," praised Arthur. His charms were definitely not working on this woman, for sure. He's definitely not her type.

"*Sulio!*" she demanded.

"You will speak when you are allowed to speak!" she instructed, with her tribal garb swishing with every heavily accented word. She wore a mask made from the skull of a beast I had never seen before and had thick, long black hair tipped red at the ends. Arthur remained silent and calm despite being seconds away from his death.

"How did you get this?" She shoved the trinket into Arthur's face and waved it frantically in front of him.

"That's mine. If you would so please release us and we will be on our way. You won't get any money off of it. It is but an old heirloom. If you do want money, it's in a brown bag over there by the horses," replied Arthur coolly.

"I don't want your useless money. I want to know how you came to possess a piece of Gabriel's soul. You are clearly not a guardian but a mere pretty village boy," she spat.

"You think I'm pretty," he smirked.

"ENOUGH!" she shouted as she inched her knife closer to his throat, nicking it just enough that a bead of blood escaped down his neck.

"Whoa, whoa, whoa. Calm down miss. His mother's a guardian. Was, a guardian. We're just following orders. We're going to Desolate Mountain to learn more of it," I replied.

"Bernard!"

"What! You're about to die and I won't let you!" I replied, while spitting out gravel and rolling over to face myself upwards. It's definitely not my proudest moment.

"Desolaia Mountagne?" she asked, but I was pretty sure it was rhetorical.

"You will die there. Turn back," she ordered.

"No, we can't. My friend and I are on a mission, although we don't know what for yet," answered Arthur.

"There is only one reason why the guardians want all of Gabriel's soul pieces back together. Something bad is going to happen and we need to resurrect our protector," she said, while slowly lowering her knife. I swear I could hear a breath of relief violently leaving me.

"We will go to my tribe at once to warn them," she continued.

"Sorry, but what are you doing out here? It's a really late night and shouldn't young, ambitious ladies like yourself be at home where it's safe?" I asked.

"Don't patronize me, you writhing worm. I'm part of the mountain guard. I could kill you in an instant. We leave, now."

Okay, now I have two people ordering me around. I might as well identify as a sheepdog from now on. She cut us loose and executed a high-pitched whistle with her fingers. A wild brown horse with no saddle galloped out of the darkness a moment later. She slips onto the horse, grabs its mane and yells at us to follow her. And so we did, like we had a choice.

***

We arrived at her village a day quicker than we thought by riding through shortcuts only known by her people. It was morning now and her garb was more elaborate than I remembered. She was definitely someone of importance in her tribe. Arthur agreed by sharing a look of awe with me. We rode in silence. There was no way Arthur and I could have found her tribe on our own. It was buried deep in the forest, inside a waterfall, that is only accessible through a cave at a certain time of day when the tides are low.

She called at the gate, and the thick, heavy wooden doors opened slowly to reveal a colorful, vibrant village decorated with ribbons of orange, blue, white, green and gray. It was definitely a sight to be remembered. Children were playing with fire, ice, and wind like how ours played with wooden toys. A blacksmith fed the furnace with his bare hands while his wife grew fresh grapes in an empty bowl. What a magical sight! We were led to the tribe leader's tent, and I was instructed to stay outside. I told them I didn't have a problem being treated as second-best but they found it hard to understand my sarcasm. I'm sure Arthur would fill me in later. I told him to have fun with Little Miss Violent and her posse while I walked off to restock on supplies.

***

I spent the whole day walking around the village, learning their language, and eating their food. They had bread that was not really bread; it was made from some sort of tree bark, but it tasted⋯ good. Better than bread even. The purple color did not faze me. The women were all dressed quite plainly compared to Little Miss Violent, but they're quite beautiful in their simplicity. I learned that the Growers dressed in bright green in homage to Gaia and their ability to wield the earth, turquoise garbs for those who wielded water, blue for ice, white for wind, orange for fire, and gray for those who wielded none. They treated grays with love though, by putting them in political positions. Apparently, visitors to this village are forbidden to leave in order to protect the village's secrets and powers. So... I'm not really sure how Arthur would react to this news when he returns from his *important* meeting.

It's taking him longer than I expected, and I've just about explored every corner of the village. It's not a large group; just about eighty to a hundred people. They're nomads, so they moved around a lot for their own safety.

A loud horn sounded and the villagers rushed to the tribe leader's tent. That was my queue. I saw Arthur, Little Miss Violent, the tribe leader, and a few other people important enough to attend the meeting leave the tent with grave looks on their faces. The tribe leader began his speech in his native tongue, solemn and slow at first, then increasing in confidence and power. I nodded and chanted at all the right places, not knowing what it was all about. Arthur and his new girlfriend walked over to me, gave me a brief summary of the speech and bestowed on me the fact that Little Miss Violent was the tribe leader's daughter. I was flabbergasted, but not surprised.

"So you mean to say that we are now sending messages to all guardians of this world to return here with a piece of Gabriel's soul so that we can put him back together to fight evil?" I asked, looking right at Little Miss Violent.

"And..." Little Miss Violent paused.

"I've been chosen to save humankind," Arthur continued.

"What? I don't understand," my eyes were frantic.

"Gabriel needs a vessel and I've volunteered, being of guardian blood. My mother was part of a lineage of Gabriel's most loyal guardians. That's why someone came to kill her. They didn't want her to be his vessel." Arthur explained.

"You can't do this." I stated in disbelief.

"I don't have a choice." Arthur replied in a low and stern voice.

"Can't Little Miss Violent do it?"

"Her name is Iowe. And no, she does not have guardian blood. It's ancestral," Arthur sighed.

"There must be another way."

"There isn't. We've discussed every other way in that tent," Arthur admitted calmly. Iowe remained silent. The tribe leader walked over to us and told us that the guardians will be arriving at their village via earth portals conjured by their Growers tomorrow morning. All six of them.

"We should get some sleep. It's a long day tomorrow," Arthur rested his hand on my shoulder before letting it fall away. Was that supposed to make me feel assured?

***

It's pouring. Hard. It's as if the world knew and was mourning its defeat in advance. The skies are beginning to turn from a dull gray to dark crimson, just as the tribe leader prophesied. No one dared speak of the evil the Angel Gabriel was supposed to protect us from. We would just have to wait and see.

One by one, the remaining six guardians climbed out of the conjured earth pods. It must have been a rather long journey, because they looked quite exhausted and covered in, well··· dirt. I wouldn't have known that they were guardians at all. They looked like regular people with regular day jobs. Arthur was dressed in the tribe's ceremonial garb and greeted each guardian warmly with a bow. Soon, four tribes of people shouldered out a rectangular golden throne laden with jewels I'd never seen before. They were in the colors of the elements, reflecting different parts of the sun. They began their ceremony with ancient songs and each guardian carefully placed their trinkets in empty slots above the throne. Once all the pieces of Angel Gabriel's soul were placed, they began to glow.

"It's time," the tribe leader announced. He guided Arthur towards the throne and motioned for him to sit. His seventh piece would be held in his right palm. For the first few moments, nothing happened. Doubt started to rise in the hearts of the people when a low thrum and pulse emanated from the throne.

The chanting intensified and the tribespeople stomped their feet to the rhythm of its pulse. Arthur began to scream and his eyes glowed white. My body reacted to save him, but I was held back by Iowe. This was not going to turn out well for my best friend. Soon, a dark crimson cloud formed above the village, and the tribespeople began to chant faster and louder. The tribe leader broke his stony expression for the first time to reveal worry and fear.

Could he awaken Angel Gabriel in time? A dark figure emerged from the cloud and its hoofed claws scratched the earth. The Growers fell to the ground as fire exploded all around the creature. They felt its rage first.

The creature said a few things that none of us could understand. Arthur, in the voice of Angel Gabriel rebuked the creature in a booming voice. Arthur's full body was glowing white now as he stood before the horned creature. He was so small compared to the creature that stood as tall as a mountain. Its fiery eyes burned the souls of anyone who looked at it, so I reminded myself to keep my eyes away from it, as I was told during training.

In the blink of an eye, both Arthur and the creature launched into the air and began their final battle. Arthur usually trusted his own oak bow in battles, but it seems like he had managed to conjure one out of thin air made of light. The lightning and thunder caused by them both were enough to shake and collapse the tribe's tents. We stood in fear, awaiting the final outcome of a battle I will never understand. Smaller versions of the creature began to pop out of the ground, and the tribespeople were doing everything they could to put the creature's minions back to where they came from. My bow and arrow took out a few. Iowe had both her knives out and was viciously slashing at them.

After a while, Arthur-Gabriel was flung into a nearby mountain, and it burst open. He launched himself back at the giant creature and shot a few more holy arrows in its direction but they kept missing. The creature was too quick. Arthur-Gabriel was losing, and I needed to do something. Not wanting to be in the middle of two celestials fighting, I figured that I could take my best shot at gathering all the tribespeople to conjure an enormous solid earth pod, big enough to hold the creature in place so that Arthur-Gabriel could have their chance.

It took all my might and courage to get the tribal leader to listen to my idea. With a blow of his horn, he gathered the most powerful tribespeople. Iowe led them. I noticed that the creature landed on the earth in intervals after attacking Arthur-Gabriel to draw power out of the earth's core. So we waited until it did, and the tribespeople worked together to put it off balance by creating a sink hole at one of its hooves and binding the feet of the gargantuan creature with all of their elements combined.

It worked.

Infuriated and feet bounded by the elements, the creature lunged a free claw at the tribe leader who was fighting nearby. Iowa put herself between her father and the creature and had herself captured instead. The creature squeezed hard and blood escaped its claws. Everything was in slow motion. A frown formed on Arthur-Gabriel's brow, and I could hear the muffled screams of the tribe leader in the background. Strung in Arthur-Gabriel's holy bow was the brightest, largest holy arrow they have made so far. He shot the finishing blow in between the creatures' eyes. The creature thundered in pain and disintegrated into ashes. In that very moment, Arthur stopped glowing and began to free-fall from the sky. The tribal leader commanded the Breezers to softly land Arthur on the ground.

Jumping over casualties and debris, I rushed over to my best friend.

Arthur was unrecognizable. And gone. The power of the Angel was too much for his mortal body to withstand. I held his body in my arms and ugly sobs followed. I could make out a small smile on his face, as if he was relieved to be finally reunited with his mother in a much better place.

"Will the creature ever come back?" I asked between heavy sobs.

"It's finished, it's not coming back. Gabriel killed it instead of imprisoning it like he did before. Gabriel need not return to us anymore," said the tribe leader.

The sky cried with me for weeks on end.

***

The village was in shambles. We buried Arthur, Iowe, and all the bodies of war in the middle of the village with a traditional tribal ceremony before relocating. As predicted, they didn't allow me to return to my village. However, I managed to fall in love and start a family here. I sent simple letters back to my village with Arthur's story, conveniently leaving out the fact that the tribe exists. Now every child born in this world will know of Arthur's story and how he saved humankind from evil.

Thank you, Arthur, for giving us a future. Main characters most often never get their happy ending. And I'm grateful I wasn't one.

The Mice and the Government

A group of mice hates the boy because the boy wants to destroy their home.
The mice are the victims.
The boy is the villain.
The boy wants to destroy the mice's nest because he wants to protect his family from disease.
The boy is a hero.
The boy wants to show that he's useful so he could be loved by his father who neglects him.
The boy is a victim.
The father is a villain.
The father has never neglected him. His son has schizophrenia and thinks that his father never loved him. His father has been caring for the boy all his life.
The father is a hero.
The father cares for his schizophrenic son and has trouble keeping a job as a single parent.
The father is a victim.
The mother is the villain.
The mother left her son and husband to fight in the war on the front lines and she can't wait to see her family again.
The mother is a hero.
The mother gets shot in the war and loses both her legs. She's losing a lot of blood but no one wants to save her. Her comrades leave her in the barracks.
The mother is a victim.
The comrades are the villains.
Her comrades left the mother in the barracks because she had provided an opening to win the fight as planned. Her comrades took it and they won.

The comrades are heroes.
The comrades won the war, but they had to be removed by the government to ensure the silence of their mission.
The comrades are the victims.
The government is the villain.
The government silenced her comrades because they had found out they were part of a dangerous resistance that could threaten the security of the country.
The government is the hero.
The government needed to prioritize its issues quickly and effectively because it was battling a plague.
The government is the victim.
The mice are the villains.
The world was getting polluted and overpopulated and the great reduction of humans on earth is helping mother earth recover.
The mice are the heroes.
Situations matter. We all want to be heroes in our own eyes.

Pseudo-immortals

"Happy 214th birthday, Sheila Patel. Here's a snapshot of your morning vitals," reported my personal female AI assistant. She does this every morning at 8am on queue. Only this time, with a *heartfelt* birthday wish. Even though recent developments have made her sound more lifelike, there's still a void, a certain kind of emptiness you could tell.

"Just another one I guess, birthdays aren't really a milestone anymore you know," I muttered.

"I detect pessimism and existentialism in your tone. Would you like me to recommend some cool new activities for you to try? Creation of milestones is fully dependent on the individual. Be better than who you were yesterday. Don't compare yo..."

"Cut the pep talk. I didn't get sarcasm and nagging mom add-ons when I got you on discount last year," I interrupted.

"I detect a level of resentment, and..."

"Detect this," I said as I switched her off with a tap on my smart watch. I breathed out a sigh of relief as I went through my daily checks on my overall body health and functionality diagnostics of my bionic right arm, two bionic legs, and my learning implant. Everything looked nice and green. Notifications popped up all around my vision wishing me happy birthday from friends and family I don't really care about. My Eyement should have been disabled. I sent an auto-reply to all the automatic birthday wishes and start my day with a cup of tea. I'd usually have my AI get one ready for me, but I chose to do it the traditional way today. For old times' sake. *Old*, what a word.

My home is covered in mirrors, like everyone else's. We're all narcissus now ever since anti-aging drugs hit the market in 2023. It seemed like ages ago. The mirrors in our homes work as interfaces too. I stared into my full reflection and thought about the life choices I have made. I'm 214 now, living alone with no family in the country, no pets, real friends and barely surviving with an AI, I'm learning to tolerate. My body is as optimal as it can be at this age, with organ replacements I can afford both to enhance my capabilities and replace the limbs I've lost in a car accident two years ago. All humans who can afford it are pseudo-immortals now, so we don't die of old age, but we're still vulnerable to nature's laws and probability. My biological makeup was frozen at 30, so I don't really have issues hitting on men younger than I am, even if they are decades my junior. My mental health is monitored closely by my company's doctors and they do keep tabs on me now and then. It's a great company benefit.

Speaking of my company, the firm I work for grows babies for Pseudos who wish to have a family. Build a Baby. I know. Not the best name. The risk of mortality from being pregnant and giving birth, both for the mother and baby are totally removed with this technology. We have a 100% success rate of births and infants who reach the age of 90. We even customize your babies too. It's an okay job, cause all I do is quality control. I know there could be more exciting things to do with your life but you don't really tell a 214 year old what to do when you know they've probably already done it all.

"Patel, let's sync up in 5," a voice message interrupted my inner monologue.

"Okay," I replied. That was Hiro Takashi, my boss. He never really sends out last minute invites unless it is absolutely vital. He's like a robot himself. Respectful, handsome and never breaks character. I looked through a few more messages and fire up a chat with Hiro.

"Good morning Hiro, what's the matter?" I asked.

"Patel! You've got to be more positive!" he exclaimed.

"Error, leadership error. Toxic positivity detected. Avoid using words like being more positive. Instead use.."

I could hear Hiro muting his AI in embarrassment before rephrasing himself. "Patel, it's your birthday! Happy birthday!" a cacophony of trumpets and violins started to play while 3D animated streamers and poppers filled my vision. My department congratulated me on being the human with the most vintage body in the company. *Vintage* is a word that replaced *old* since our bodies are treated like artifacts now.

"We don't know what drives you to want to live this long in that vintage body of yours Patel, but oh damn! Tell us your secrets! Do you have a private psychologist motivating you? Is it love?" inquired a colleague.

"She probably hasn't tried everything on this earth yet, Summer. Everyone has a list."

I cut their speculation off with a quick 'thank you' and urged them all to get back to work, even though technically it was Hiro's job to do so.

Love. The word lingered on in my mind throughout the workday.

***

After dinner I spent all night rereading texts on all the types of love and researching its definition. I came across a poem written by a Malaysian poet, Charissa Ong Ty centuries ago. It was titled, The Nature of Love.

Love is difficult to understand,
Yet, so simple to know.
Love is many things.
Love is an emotion.
Love lives in affection, sacrifice, devotion,
selflessness, passion, respect, and loyalty.

Love is a connection.
Love is romantic, patriotic, biochemical, egotistical,
familial, theological, materialistic or friendly.
Love exists in all of them,
or sometimes, within none at all.
I thank love for all of its facets,
and centuries of illogical mysteries,
love can belong to all who breathe,
but it can also solely belong to me.

From that list, I dove deep into romance, patriotism, family, and friendly love. I compared and analyzed which love had the least risks, best outcomes, and longevity. If I needed love, I needed it to last, especially if it was going to be for another few hundred years. After a few all nighters of research, I've come to a conclusion.

I need a baby.

Nothing is stronger than a mother-child familial bond. As history suggests.

***

The following morning, I sent a nervous message to human resources asking them if there were any employee benefits to those who wish to build their own baby. He was ecstatic as he should be, and shared me the details. It was expensive still, even with the measly 15% employee discount. I put in a deposit and went through the catalog via the app.

Use your own genetic material or otherwise? Hazel or brown eyes? Tall or medium tall? Athletic or studious? If you check studious, there is a 10% discount on all learning implants. Reference for bone structure? *Please upload an image here.* Skin, cool tones or warm tones?

I checked cool tones and a little tooltip popped up beside it.

We do not allow customisation of skin color at this time due to inclusivity laws. All babies will be born brown temporarily.

Honestly, brown was perfect.

I clicked submit and waited for my receipt and confirmation. In a few moments, my AI informed me that my baby will be ready in 5 months. It's real. It's really happening!

I kept myself busy by taking up new hobbies and preparing our home for the little one. I even came up with a few name options.

***

Five months have passed and my baby was ready. I've learned that she was a girl the moment the birth pod detected it a month into production. It was so exciting. I'm thankful that Build a Baby left this as an element of surprise. Genders were given at random and were fully customisable when children reached adolescence. I offered to quality check my baby, but Hiro said it was a conflict of interest. So, he had Summer do it instead. He allowed me to end work early to prepare for my newborn, but not without the barrage of trumpets and streamers.

Rocking back and forth on the balls of my feet I waited for my doorbell to ring. It's more than the occasional package delivery. It's not just some temporary high. It's responsibility, hurt, and joy all rolled into one.

It was three hours past the expected delivery and my baby hadn't arrived. I called the delivery service and the people at my company to check, but it seems like she was still in transit. My worry intensified. Just when I began my meditation exercises to calm myself down, the doorbell rang.

The delivery man handed my daughter over to me carefully. She was in mint condition and so beautiful. I was so glad I opted for post baby delivery. I wouldn't want to puncture the sac myself and clean it all up after just for the 'bespoke' experience. I thanked the delivery man with a small beep tip and brought her in. Her coo-ing was the most beautiful sound I've ever heard and my love for her overflowed.

My AI assisted me in most of the technicalities so it wasn't too hard being a mother for the first time. Her learning implant was activated as soon as she reached a month old and she was talking in the following two. Beautiful dark hair flowed down her neck and brown eyes sparkled with intensity. My little Shiva Patel. You are everything to me.

***

"Happy 244th birthday mom!!"

She grew up and became an intelligent, athletic, beautiful young woman. Something that I could definitely take credit for. She brought over a little breakfast tray with a cheese omelet, orange juice and some grapes. She stuck a tiny candle in the omelet because she knew how much I detest cakes.

"Thank you dear." I blew out the candle and checked my watch for my vitals. Everything looks OK, as usual.

"Want to go to a party this weekend to celebrate? I have some cute friends," she winked.

"Shiva, I'm done with dating decades ago. I'm happy. Complete," I replied. Shiva has almost reached an optimal age to begin preservation and anti-ageing. We look more like sisters now than mother and daughter. "It's your 30th birthday soon too, Shiva. We need to get you to the preservation center," I reminded.

"Yup, right after this weekend's party, ok?"

"Anything for you, darling. But just this once. And because it's your birthday, not mine." My daughter squeals with delight and disappears to her room to start picking out outfits for us.

***

The music was so loud. I thank my AI for pre-purchasing party ear plugs for me as soon as Shiva suggested the party. We're dressed to the nines, and the alcohol is starting to kick in.

"Mom there's someone I want you to meet," she yelled over the music and dragged me by the arm to a corner of the club where a young looking gentleman sat.

"Enchanté, my name is Johan Murrs," he said as he offered his bionic hand. "Nice to meet you, I'm Shiela," I replied as I gave him a firm shake.

"Mom, Johan is around the same age as you, and he's vintage too!"

"Oh really?" he asked.

"Yes, really," I answered.

Shiva retreated to rejoin her friends and left me with the stranger. Flirting was so not in my nature anymore, but I guess it wouldn't hurt to make a few more friends. We talked and laughed for hours. I found myself getting lost in his beautiful face. I knew it was purchased, but damn, did he have good taste. As the clock struck 12am, I politely excused myself to search for my daughter to wish her happy 30th birthday.

I couldn't find her. She was missing.

Her friends didn't know where she was or who she was with before her disappearance. My heart thumped loudly with the music and my head got lighter as the seconds flew by. I was getting frantic alarms and notifications from my heart rate monitor but I couldn't care less. I had to find her. I pushed dancing bodies aside to clear a path to the exit of the club, and fired up my personal device. She couldn't have gotten far. I've avoided doing this the whole time I was raising her to avoid looking like a helicopter parent but there's just no other way. The blinking light on my device showed me where my daughter was heading to but it went dim immediately after. Rage consumed me as I summoned a nearby car to take me to her previous known location.

The Good Samaritan dropped me by a dark alleyway. I found my daughter's body lying on the ground faced down. Everything inside of me liquified, my breath stopped, and my world crumbled. I inched closer to inspect her when a police officer stopped me in my tracks.

"Ma'am, we've got a crime scene here. I suggest that you do not go any further," the officer stated.

"She's my daughter!!" The delayed tears from shock finally came and I screamed for an ambulance. Later, the officer told me that he had already called for one. Out of sympathy, he let me go to my daughter.

Her body was in pristine condition. But upon checking her vitals on her smart watch, it showed numerous cancers blowing up all over her body once the clock struck 12am. How could this happen? Who murdered my child?

***

Back home, I downloaded all her health data and compiled it as evidence. I was investigating Shiva's murder, planning her funeral and mourning her all at once. It was the hardest time of my 244 years of life. Johan called me a few times to ask how I was doing but I couldn't bear to talk to anyone. At least not now. I drew maps on walls and tried to find relationships between each possible culprit. Was it my company? Did they mess up? They couldn't. It's a multi-billion dollar business, they couldn't have let a faulty product escape their premises. Was it Summer? She was supposed to do quality checks on Shiva. But she had no qualms against me, at least none that I know of. It was leading nowhere.

"Sheila Patel, your bionic arm model R234X-2 will be discontinued soon. Would you like to purchase a replacement?" distracted my AI. "Not now, AI." And I buried myself further into the case.

***

I stood before the large white doors of Bionic Technologies, with a folder in hand. This is it, I thought to myself. Now, I will bring my daughter's death to justice. It has been two years since.

"I'm here to meet Dr. Hoover Mathers, I'm a journalist for Bionics Weekly. He's expecting me," I lied. The receptionist looked at me blankly and took half a minute to check the Doctor's appointments on her little handheld device.

"It looks like he is. Please, this way, Miss Preta," said the receptionist.

I managed to hack into Preta the Journalist's calendar when I heard her boasting in Starbucks about the interview hour she will have with the world's top bionic experts this weekend. 'IMDBEST123' is not a secure password. I removed the invite from her calendar just in case. She was also boasting about the hundreds of interviews she had scheduled that week, so missing one could be an easy oversight.

I walked confidently passed security checks and guards until I arrived at Dr. Hoover's lab.

"You have one hour. Please take the elevator back to the ground floor when you're done," reminded the receptionist. I watched her go, leaving me alone with Dr. Hoover.

"Hello," I said, breaking the silence.

Dr. Hoover was hunched over a bionic heart when he saw me walked in. "Ah, the R234X-2, you should probably get that replaced. And soon. If you still want an arm," he said, while scanning the rest of my body.

"Doctor, I have a few questions for you."

"Go on, you have the hour. Make sure I look good," he winked, and went back to work.

I tried my best to calm my nerves and mustered every ounce of courage I had.

"Is it true that you sabotaged Build a Baby's gene lab to kill off all future adults just when they turn 30 so that you can make sure only vintage bodies are alive and dependant on your technology? I know you're blaming it on BAB's faulty products and incompetence." I've rehearsed this monologue too many times.

"What? That's preposterous. Where did you hear that?"

"You knew babies built after Model 23AX, my Shiva, would have perfect bodies that had the potential for organ regrowth and wouldn't need your bionics anymore. Is it true?"

"Quite an advancement indeed. Organ regrowth." He stopped what he was doing for a moment as if he were about to say something else, but stopped to continue his work on his project.

"I have here in my hand, evidence of gene tempering at Build a Baby two years ago. Confess. Doctor." My hands shook, but I said it in confidence anyway.

He put his soldering iron down calmly and turned his body to face me. I could feel the ice in his stare freezing my entire body.

"What is your name again, young lady?" he asked, slowly and carefully.

"Sheila Patel," I said, with the tremor in my voice clear.

"Now you listen here very closely, Sheila. Go back to where you came from and I highly suggest you let the big boys deal with big boy problems, do you understand? There is literally nothing you can do. Build a Baby is history," he smirked and snatched my folder out of my hands. With a tap of a button, two guards came in to escort me out of his lab. My rage was apparent, and he relished it.

What he didn't know was that I had instructed my AI to send the recording of our conversation to every news station known to man. She helped translate and transcribe it too, attaching all evidence to the document. The only way I could get a recording device into his lab was if I was a journalist, so that was an easy loophole to exploit.

Weeks later, Dr. Hoover and his colleagues were arrested for trespassing, violation of human rights, and murder. I lost my bionic arm and my legs were next. Bionics were a dying technology anyway and the company I used to get them from technically did not exist anymore. I mean, I could risk it by getting new ones off the black market but I wouldn't risk an infection or a hacking.

Rolling around in my wheelchair, my quality of life deteriorated. Although I could not move around as much as I liked anymore, I was content. Shiva will always be in my heart, and her murder as with many others have been brought to justice.

After many rounds of discussions with my psychologists, friends and family, I've finally decided that it was time to go. I guess 246 is the age Sheila Patel leaves earth.

Finally happy and full of love.

The panda and the red panda

During particularly warm days at the Zoo, you can find Panda and Red Panda cooling themselves on a block of ice. They love to lick it too, like a treat. After a few moments of quiet relaxation, a family with two children walked over to admire both pandas in their respective enclosures. The children were confused as to why the pandas shared a name but looked completely different. One is black and white and has a short tail, while the other has red fur and a long striped tail. There was a little friendly debate between the two young children before they left to visit the cheetahs further down the path.

"Are we both pandas?" asked the red panda.

"I'm afraid so," replied the panda.

"But why are you afraid?" asked the red panda once more.

"One of us must be real, and the other not. We look different but we have the same name. There should be only one of us, or it will be confusing, won't it?"

"Do you think I'm imaginary?" asked the red panda.

"No··· but I'd like to think so. Because if you're not real, I shouldn't be here talking to you. People would think that I'm crazy, talking to nobody." The panda frowned.

"I think we're both real," pondered the red panda.

"How sure are you?" questioned the panda.

"I'm pretty sure. We both have information boards with brief details about us at the front of our enclosure. We kind of exist because other people gave us evidence to believe that we do," answered the red panda, but he himself was unsure.

"So is everything I am reduced to what is stated on the board and what other people or animals make us out to be?" asked the panda.

"Words can mean many things, you know. You are not who you are because people tell you who to become," claimed the red panda.

"But if they don't call me a Panda, what should I call myself?" the panda rolled over on his ice block.

"Anything you want to be, really," the red panda replied.

"That's confusing and difficult. So if I can't know if I exist, and if I can't depend on others giving me evidence that I exist···" the panda trailed off sadly.

"It can be quite an adventure. Finding out who you want to be. People, your environment, and all the other animals can help you figure that out too. But you call all the shots in the end." the red panda exclaimed joyfully.

"Like you. You're helping me figure out who I am, red panda. Do you know who you want to be?" the panda asked inquisitively.

"Nope. And that's okay. I'm taking my time," the red panda bared his teeth into a smile.

"So are you fine with us being both pandas and confusing the animals and people around us?"

"I think they should want to learn about us, notice the little unique differences and appreciate them. We don't have to change a thing," said the red panda.

"True. Well, there is one thing that everyone can agree on is, we're both adorable!" laughed the Panda.

"That, I can agree on," smiled the Red Panda rolling over with content.

Ultiaria Motives

Sky. My mother told me that even though I was a child of the sea, she could see the whole universe in my eyes. She loved it when they turned gold in the sun, or how they glowed luminescent in the dark, and gray when it rains. A piece of the sky was always with her, giving her hope that she could one day grow wings to fly far away from our seabed. Unfortunately, that was where she went. The other merpeople did not like her way of thought, but sympathized anyway when she passed from a known merdisease, Merpox. There was no cure and it infects one out of three hundred merfolk. The disease became apparent when a new dangerous chemical factory was built a few kilometers away from our underwater city, Ultiaria. My brother, Julius, is the only family I have left and is a survivor of the disease. However, it left him disabled. His decapitated fin made it difficult for him to swim and he depended on me to take care of the both of us. As for my father, we don't remember him. I was told that he left the day my brother was born. I was only three.

"Sky, you have a customer," my brother paged. I read the message on the flashing LED and let the customer in with the beep of a button. I tapped on the light button twice to let my brother know I was aware, while working on an earring piece for Madame Turquisha. Seconds later, I felt a tap on my shoulder interrupting my flow.

"My darling Sky!" she signed.

"Aunt Rachel! You're not supposed to be here until the next whale migration, which is like, in two months? What brings you over so quickly?" She enveloped me in a tight hug before I could even finish signing. I could see Julius floating into my workshop from the corner of my eye with a grin on his face. Although we weren't blood-related, we loved Aunt Rachel all the same. She was our mother's best friend.

"Oh, it's a secret, urgent business Sky. The underwater world is changing. King Poseidon is about to sign a treaty with the land people to stop building factories around our cities! I'm working as their interpreter this weekend. Shh, don't tell anyone," smirked Aunt Rachel. Her signing was so quick I could hardly keep up.

"It's not very much a secret now isn't it?" I laughed and large bubbles escaped me.

"But it's great news! Hopefully, the disease will... cease!" Aunt Rachel twirled.

All three of us were grinning at each other and we hugged a bone-crushing hug one more time.

"I have presents from the Eastern current. Come. Julius, I have something very special for you," motioned Aunt Rachel while giving a quick glance at Julius' stump of flesh where his fin used to be.

"Presents!" Julius piped up immediately and followed our Aunt to her sunken cart.

***

"I wonder how Aunt Rachel's meeting is going... It's today, isn't it? They're having it by the shore near our city?" Julius had a permanent crease forming above his brow now, aging him.

"I hope the land people do the right thing. King Poseidon doesn't take injustice lightly," I signed him through my tool shelves while testing out a few hair clips I designed. I looked at myself in the mirror and admired the shimmer the pearls were refracting off. They match my dark blue locks perfectly, but not so much my client's. I'm thinking if I should keep them and use another set of stones for her instead.

I feel a sigh of bubbles behind me.

"Stop worrying Julius, it's going to be fine," I gestured. As though fate was ever ready to prove me wrong, a siren blares. Its vibrations and blinding light fill my workshop and the rest of the city.

"What's happening?" eyes frantic, Julius awaited my next order.

"We have to get to safety. Now!" I signaled.

***

Although disabled, Julius could still swim quicker than I ever could because of his very well-made bionic fin Aunt Rachel got him a few days ago. His new fin and he were inseparable. I held on tight and directed him through a mess of panicked merfolk and sea friends. Speaking of sea friends... Olga!

"Oh no, we have to warn Olga. She's an outcast and she's too far out to hear the warnings!" I signal to my brother to swim out to the deep water caves where Olga was residing. He nodded. Olga is one of my only friends that have stuck with me since childhood. She got in trouble for something big and she never talks about it. A few moments later, we reached her cave to find her already packing.

"Olga! We need to go!" I urged.

"I know Sky, I hooked up an alert sensor at the city's emergency center so I could tell if there's an emergency. I'm not dumb," she smiled while she signed.

"But I can't find sanctuary with you. I'm an outcast, remember?" she tapped the side of her forehead as an emphasis.

"Everyone is panicking right now, no one will notice. You have to come with us!" my signs were getting more messy and indecipherable now.

"Don't worry Sky, get your brother to safety and I'll ping you once I'm safe. I'm going to find my uncle. Here's a communication device I made. We'll chat in Morse, for safety. It translates to every other language that exists in this world too. I know, I'm a genius. See ya Sky, Julius." She packed up the last of her things and swam off quicker than I could put the bulky device on. My wrist felt heavy now but it will have to do. It definitely needed some accessorizing when we get back to my workshop. If, we get back to my workshop.

***

Julius and I arrived at the Merbunker set up by Poseidon's guard decades ago. I never thought that we would be using it today. Thousands of merfolk and sea friends squeezed shoulder to shoulder and fin to fin.

"What happened on the shore?" I signed to the guard. He stood firm and remained expressionless. We waited for six more hours with booms exploding overhead. Is there a war? The device remained silent, and I sent a silent prayer for Olga. Rumors spread like barnacles by merfolk who were trying to desperately make sense of everything that was going on. My brother and I refused to believe any of them.

Soon, a giant holograph of King Poseidon shimmered to life at the center of the bunker.

"My people," King Poseidon signed.

"There is a war with the land people. A rogue bullet shot one of our interpreters and broke the peace treaty. We will fight to defend our honor. Please stay put and be safe. We will let you know when it's time to emerge. That is all." And with that, the screen blipped black. It took five whole seconds for everyone in the bunker to process the message before exploding into complete hysteria. The guards were executing desperate measures to control the crowd.

"Shot one of the interpreters? Was it Aunt Rachel?" Julius signed, frowning.

"I hope not. Let's make sure of it." I replied, and guided Julius to one of the loose vents I spotted just a minute ago. One of the screws looked shaky, and I knew I could get it open with one of my Kanzashis. We leveraged on the commotion to distract the guards, and slipped through the vents out to the open sea.

***

The device Olga gave me worked like a locator too. I navigated while my brother took us toward the shore at triple the speed. We were lucky that his fins were powered kinetically so that it would never likely die, unlike all our machines in our city. It was a long two-hour journey that felt like five hours. The skies were thick with smoke and there were falling pieces of flying machines. The sea was littered with floating debris and bodies. Their blood turned our turquoise sea deep red. My brother and I exchanged a look of horror. It was impossible to breathe both in the water and out of it. The Royal Merguards were shooting jets of water at the land guards and got shot by guns in return. It was a massacre. We stayed low behind large floating debris to avoid being seen while we scanned the shore for our aunt. A large tidal wave directed our attention to King Poseidon fighting against a large warship in the distance. A few moments later they retreated into the water. I was confused. How could they? King Poseidon and his guards could easily sink a building with the amount of power that they had.

My brother and I swam closer to shore when a loud bang threw us out of the water. There was ringing in my ears, and my vision was temporarily impaired. I screamed for my brother, but I could not find him. In one last desperate attempt, I fought against the waves with my tired limbs, and fins but it only drained me more of my blood. My world soon faded to black.

***

Murmurs and hushed voices woke me up from the darkness as I tried to make out the bodily shapes in front of me. Everything was a blur, lights too bright, sounds too sharp. I could only recognize faint mechanical sounds, slightly different from the muffled ones from my city. Someone made a startled noise. They were probably alerting the rest of my awakening. I drifted back to sleep.

***

"Hhhhlllo," said a voice. It was human. My panicked eyes widened, and I attempted to run. I realized shortly afterwards that my arms were restrained. I was afraid, angry, and confused. My lungs gave out a loud shriek for help to my people, but it just reverberated helplessly around the white room. The man in a white coat, whom I assumed was a human doctor from my studies of human culture, turned a knob on my device.

"Forgive me, I must have forgotten to switch on your translator. It's quite a good build, I must say. Old, but good. Reminds me of the one we have here on land," the doctor said.

I understood every word. I wanted to scream at him not to touch me, or his head would be on a hunting stick, but I couldn't. My hands were restrained and I couldn't sign.

"Is she mute, doctor?" A man in a smart suit asked.

"Merpeople use sign language to communicate. Unfortunately, we've made her so by restraining her. We'll wait a few more days for close observation before *talking* to her, General," the doctor implied.

"She's wearing a TRX160 device. Haven't seen one of those in a long time," the smart suit man also known as General said.

"Teach her to speak and walk. We need her in the war efforts. She seems... intelligent. And if she turns out to be who we think she is..." his voice trailed off as his ice-blue eyes gave me a quick glance into his frozen soul. I have to watch out for this man.

"Alright, see you General Adkins, let the merlady have her rest." bid the doctor. The General marched out without a word.

"Okay merlady, I'd love to speak with you but I need to be sure that I'll be safe, okay? So I'm strapping this electric shocker on your left leg here... to..." his voice drifted off into inaudible noises when I noticed two meaty legs instead of my beautiful blue-green luminescent fin. The sudden realization put me into a rage once more and I began screaming for King Poseidon to come save me.

"Merlady, you're on land now, far, far away from the sea. No one will come for you. Please, cooperate," he said while locking in the electric ankle cuff with great difficulty.

"Please, if you do anything dangerous, I'll shock you. So don't do anything unexpected. It's linked to my heart rate monitor too. So it's important you keep me really calm," warned the doctor.

I nodded. He unrestrained my arms and I let blood flow back into them. My legs felt odd like they weren't mine to use. Thoughts shifted to my brother, Aunt Rachel, and Olga. He took a few breaths with me and made sure my breathing was slow. I was furious, but leveled.

"Alright, first question, what is your name?" the doctor signed.

I was surprised that he could, so I signed for Sky.

"Sky?" he signed. His brow furrowed.

"No, you're The Technologist," he re-emphasized. I signed no and signed for Sky once more.

"Ah, this is going to be a little more difficult than I thought," he muttered to himself.

"This device on your wrist. Is it yours?" he asked. I signed yes and told him nothing more. I wasn't going to put anyone else in danger. "Thank you, Sky. We will resume tomorrow with some language and remembering lessons. Rest well." He paused before leaving.

"Oh, I'm sorry I must have forgotten to introduce myself, how rude of me. I'm Doctor March. Like the month. I'll be working with you these coming months. Hopefully, to help you regain your memory," he continued, verbally. My device beeped in response, almost saying that it had reached the maximum amount of words to be translated today.

When he left, I heard a latch and lock on the door. I tried everything to break off the electric cuff but it was indestructible. I trashed the room. The nurse who brought my meals had a face that was rid of emotion. Something tells me that mistreatment of patients occurred quite often here. She had a little remote control too, ready to zap me the moment she notices a sliver of misbehavior.

***

I spend the next few days plotting my escape while Doctor March tries to get me to remember something I seem to have forgotten. Land people's language started to form clumsily from my lips, and my legs grew more muscular from all the walking and running they were making me do. I was thankful that the thick curvature of my body and tanned skin remained, although my fin did not. How did that happen? I wonder. The worst thing about all of this was when they put me in land people's clothes. My chest protruded, and my waist was cinched so tight that I could hear the belt popping open. The nurses told me I was beautiful and styled my blue hair in large, wavy curls that reminded me of the sea I missed so much.

My meals mostly consist of seaweed, which is my favorite, as well as fish and crab. Fruits and land meat were odd, so I avoided them at all costs. The General comes in to check on me from time to time, telling the Doctor to do his job or he'll lose it. My hatred for him grows everyday, just like the tension between my people and theirs at this moment. The news told me that we are in a cold war now, but I know both sides are intensely planning their next move of attack.

***

I was sketching a few jewelry designs beside portraits of my brother one afternoon in the common room when the General walked in.

"Sky? Is that your real name?" asked the General.

"Yes. It is." I replied with my limited knowledge of English. He flashed his translator and told me that it was safe to sign. He had to stand a little bit further away so that the camera on his translator could capture my gestures well. I'm glad about the tech limitations. I didn't want him any closer than he was now.

"Have you remembered anything from your past?" he asked.

"All I know is that I'm just a regular merlady from Ultiaria. I have no family, and I am not this technologist you speak of," I signed. It took a while for his device to translate. His eyes drifted to the portrait of my brother, and I hid it away immediately.

"Who is that?"

"Somebody."

"Who?" he inched closer, and I swear we were exchanging breaths for a moment. He was so intense, and I hated him all the more. I glared back uncomfortably until he decided to back away first. Good boy.

"General Adkins. What a surprise," interrupted Doctor March.

"How's progress? It's been two months."

"She's extremely intelligent, sir. Picked up our language and poised..."

"I'm talking about her memory. Not her tuition, Doctor. I need intel. Now." The General was growing impatient. The Doctor motioned him away from me, but I could still hear their muffled conversation.

"Don't you think we might have abducted the wrong merlady? Just an idea," the Doctor proposed nervously.

"She knows something. I know she's linked to The Technologist. Try harder," demanded the General. The Doctor nodded in defeat.

***

It was in the middle of the night right after my salt water bath when I heard my device beeping. It wasn't the regular, I'm-loading-your-translation-beep. It was Morse code. Olga! I grabbed my notebook and scribbled down the message immediately.

I-M-S-A-F-E-Y-O-U

I sent her back a message by tapping on the sole button on the device.

T-R-A-P-P-E-D-L-A-N-D-P-P-L

I sent her another message almost immediately, without waiting for a reply.

T-E-C-H-N-O-L-O-G-I-S-T-W-H-O

She made me wait a long while before sending me a reply.

I-M-C-O-M-I-N-G

She's coming? How? Of course, my device had a tracker. But I'm sure the land people removed it while I was asleep though. Removing all doubt of Olga's capabilities, I smiled. Finally, someone was coming to save me.

***

I showed no hint of my brief conversation with Olga last night the next morning during Doctor March's daily checkups. My heart was beating like a drum as it anticipated a rescue from my best friend. The General was an odd man. He came to watch me sketch without saying anything. Half of me thinks that he's genuinely interested in art, but the other half of me thinks that he's just waiting to see more evidence from my past.

"Why are you here every day, General? What do you expect to see?" I asked nervously, still facing the window. My English was as fluent and native as it could be. He didn't answer right away.

"Nothing." The bone-dry answer irked me to the core so much that when I swung around to face him, his hand was already poised to pick up my fallen pencil. I took it from his hands without muttering a word of thanks. We shared a few moments of awkward silence before my device started beeping in Morse Code again. He noticed it immediately, and he lunged for my wrist. Anger mixed with concern lit up his eyes.

"Who are you contacting? What is it for?" he demanded. His grip on my wrist was so tight that I could no longer feel my fingers.

"Nothing," I stood up and looked him point blank in the eye.

Moments later, there was a loud explosion at the far end of the common room that threw the General and I backwards. His body shielded me from the incoming glass shards from the windows.

"Sky!" Olga yelled.

"Olga!!" I was so happy to see her.

"What of my brother? Is he alright?" I signed.

"He's fine. He's safe and worried sick about you. You look horrible," she signed while scanning me from head to toe. I groaned in response.

The General was still trying to recover from the blast, but he managed to call for assistance anyway.

"We need to go."

"Right." I took one glance back at the General and left with Olga.

I followed her lead and jumped over fences and bushes, only to find a black SUV parked in the middle of nowhere. I find it odd that Olga was able to use her legs so effortlessly.

"That's our ride," she said. We jumped in, and our driver sped up so quickly that we were thrown to the back of the car.

"Olga, there's something you're not telling me. Truth. Now. Are you even from our city?" I demanded while trying to balance myself.

"Yes, I am. Was. Until the King outcasted me. I was the technologist. I built the most advanced machines for Ultiaria and advanced the mersociety light years ahead of their time. But a betrayer from my workshop took my designs and sold them to the land people, revealing all the vulnerabilities of our city. The King thought I was behind it all yada yada yada... old story," she signed it all so quickly that I barely caught all of it.

"Olga! Why haven't you told me this?!"

"My identity was a secret, and anyone who knew me could be used as leverage. Like you."

I grunted in frustration and forced myself to believe her story. I had no time to doubt because we had land people with guns on our tails. Figuratively, of course. Our tails have somewhat gone missing, and we don't know why or how we can get them back.

"Surrender now or we will not hesitate to shoot," a voice over a speaker blared from one of the police cars behind us.

"Lose them!" Olga instructed the driver. Only, there wasn't anyone sitting in the driver's seat. I should've known that she built this car too. We swerved, and jumped over railings, and destroyed cones while avoiding flying bullets.

"Sky, we have your brother. Surrender now, or he will die. You have 10 seconds to comply."

I shared a look of absolute shock with Olga. How?

"I've changed my mind. I don't like waiting." We heard a gunshot.

"I've got your Aunt Rachel now. I'm giving you another 10 seconds." I couldn't recognize the voice, but it certainly wasn't the Generals. Olga did a quick check on Julius's vitals remotely via her device and noticed that his heartbeat was no longer there. Rage filled the both of us, and Olga instructed the car to turn around. She pulled out two grenade launchers from under her seat, and aimed them at the car with the speakers, and fired. The car exploded into a thick cloud of smoke, and its debris rolled over and crashed into the other police car that was in pursuit of us. Our SUV car spun 180 degrees and was driving at full speed towards the city bridge.

The car burst through the barricades and landed deep into the seawater. Our legs transformed into fins again in the worst possible pain imaginable. I was blessed that I was knocked out cold when it happened the other way around.

"We need to finish this, Olga. I'm done running away. They killed Julius." I signed. Olga pondered for a moment before darkening her expression.

"Then let's do it. Eat this. I've been saving this for emergencies. It's from my uncle." She clicked open her wrist device and offered me a glowing red pill from it. Without hesitation, I swallowed it with a mouthful of seawater. I felt myself biologically morphing into something larger and stronger.

Who, or what was I turning into? Power coursed through my veins and I could feel the obedience and anticipation of all creatures of the deep. I burst out of the water, now having three fins instead of one, and four wings that sprouted from my spine granting me the ability to fly. Mother would be proud. I laughed maniacally with tears in my eyes as I was still grieving my dead brother. I conjured waves that swallowed cars, houses and pulled helicopters from the sky. The land people tried to quell my rage but it felt like nothing could stop me. The fire in me boiled hot like lava. Looking down, I soon identified the General. He was armed with a shotgun. He put it down slowly and stared deep into my eyes as if asking for a truce. It's those piercing blue eyes again.

I raised my hand ready to strike but held it there for a moment. He was signing for me to stop and talk. From the corner of my eye, I could see King Poseidon making his way from the horizon to either join me or stop me, I don't know. I refocused my goal to destroy the land people once and for all. They deserved all of this. They have killed so many of our people all these years. If the King can't finish the job, I'll gladly do it instead. I scanned the waters for Olga but she was nowhere to be found. The sea was stained red once more. A moment of terror was apparent in my eyes as King Poseidon raised his golden trident toward me and the city.

Why did Olga do this to me? Am I but her puppet or her weapon of justice?

***

This story was part of a challenge where I got my friend YZ to fill in my template with random stuff and I had to make a story out of it. This was the template I created. Try it, it's fun.

Character
Species: Merhuman
Gender: Girl
Appearance: 7, blue hair, plus sized, curvy
Character: Reserved, Shy
Social Status: Average, wallflower
Antihero/Hero/Side character: villain
Family construct: Orphan, younger brother she will protect at all costs
Friend construct: Outcast
Hobbies: Jewelry making
Hates: People who are overly nice
Goals: disabled brother to be happy
Weaknesses/Strengths: Her brother
Era: Future
Trusty sidekick: none
Favorite food: seaweed
Romantic interest: Yes
Forbidden?: Yes

Story
Theme: Relationship/Family
Genre: Fantasy/Dystopian
Ending: Cliff hanger

Thank yous

Has it been 7 years since I launched Midnight Monologues? It has been such a crazy ride! First and foremost, I would like to thank the thousands of readers who have seen value in my work. I could never thank you enough for your endless support and love.

I'd like to thank my family for everything. Especially to my mom, Alina Wong for being the best logistics/accountant/HR person in the world. I promise I'll pay you better this year. *laughs* I'd like to thank the interns and staff who contributed so much to the company. You all were and are still so amazing. Many thought we are a large company, but we are simply just three with the efficiency of twenty. It didn't stop us from being one of the top independent publishing houses in Malaysia. I take pride in that, and in you.

The poetry and book community is growing in Malaysia, and I am so happy that it is. I remembered putting this precise goal in the Vision and Mission board when I started Penwings Publishing in 2016.

And finally, in the words of Snoop, I'd like to thank me too, for keeping up the consistency of publishing myself and others. I had so many reasons to give up but I'm glad I didn't. I'm so happy to where it brought me. You know what, I think I'll book myself a nice little trip somewhere to treat myself. :)

About the author

Charissa Ong Tse Ying is born and bred in Subang Jaya, Malaysia, 1992. With a career in Interactive Media Design, she juggles between her two passions, designing and writing— nurturing both like a growing child. The past seven years have been filled with amazing interactions and events with all her readers. She never knew that she would be in this industry for this long. Charissa is quite apologetic for publishing her third book five years after her second one and blames it on the various hobbies she loves distracting herself with. She thanks you for taking your time to read her stories, your continuous support, and enthusiasm in sharing them with your friends and family. She wants you to know that you are so appreciated.

fb.com/cotypoems
@cotypoems on Instagram

Goodreads/CharissaOngTy
(Do drop a review and rating, it will help so much!)

Books by Penwings

MIDNIGHT MONOLOGUES

By Charissa Ong Ty

No.1 Best-Selling English Poetry and Short Stories is sold in major bookstores in Malaysia, Singapore and the Philippines. #MidnightMonologues is divided into four parts: LOST, FOUND, HOPE, and Short Stories. In an age of decreased readership and short attention spans, this book aims to ignite the readers' imagination; with short, melodious writing.

DAYLIGHT DIALOGUES

By Charissa Ong Ty

Back by popular demand, Charissa Ong Ty's second Poetry and Short Stories book, #DaylightDialogues, re-explores heartbreak, deep aspirations of love, self-actualization and fictional short stories.

Pushing her boundaries with more challenging technical poetry writing, she hopes her readership would appreciate Daylight Dialogues as much as they did Midnight Monologues.

Books by Penwings

QUESTIONS TO OUR ANSWERS
By Timothy Joshua

#QTOA is a poetry and fiction book containing three main chapters, centred around questions one would ask during different stages of a relationship: What are we? Where are we going? How are we getting there? The poems, juxtaposed with short stories, take readers on a deeply reflective journey as they contemplate the deepest thoughts and hopes they carry for their past and present relationships.

MORE THAN WORDS
By Zack Shah

A diary, a love letter and a storybook all rolled into one, Zack Shah bares it all in his debut poetry collection. #MTW is a collection where each page is a small window into a world where reality and imagination are childhood friends. From the innocence of young romance to the dangers of desire, experience the entire spectrum of human emotion laced in between his crafted words.

**POETRY & SHORT STORIES -
A PRACTICE BOOK**
By Charissa Ong Ty

The Penwings Practice Book is a short story and poetry activity book authored by Best-Selling author Charissa Ong Ty. She has included her entire thought process and technical writing methods in this book to help you realize your writing career! If you are thinking of picking up writing as an interest, the Penwings Practice Book provides great fundamental learnings that can be practiced individually or in a classroom setting.

A STRANGE AND WICKED MAGIC
By Zack Shah

A dark but familiar sequel to the best-selling "More than Words", Zack Shah returns with a much-anticipated second volume of poetry and prose titled "A Strange and Wicked Magic".

Haunting, beautiful, and provocative, this new collection unravels the ambivalent nature of love, how it is neither good nor bad but both: venom and nectar, poison and cure, heaven and hell. This book will take you through the highs and lows of it all, the pain and the pleasure, the chaos and the calm, the hurting and the healing. A bittersweet read for the lovelorn, the lonely, and the lost.

GENERATION OF FRAGILE

By Germaine Thai

A showcase of the phases and moments in life, many of which are simple but beautiful. The book is a collection of inspirations and realizations from the past decade; the uncertainty that comes with getting lost in the early 20s, coupled with the maturity that comes from finding slight wisdom in the late 20s. We are a generation protected from many hardships, which in turn makes us fragile when life throws us curveballs. These words reassure that it is okay to be broken. It hopes to offer companionship to every reader's journey to becoming whole again.

NOT QUITE ALONE

By Tasha Lim

Not Quite Alone serves as a poignant introduction to the emotional rollercoaster within its pages. Readers are invited to delve into a world where unfamiliar emotions are laid bare, inviting a sense of connection and shared humanity. As the pages unfold, it becomes evident that the feelings explored here are not isolated experiences but universal threads that bind us all.

MIDNIGHT MONOLOGUES AUDIOBOOK
By Charissa Ong Ty

Midnight Monologues Audiobook has two renditions. A female reader and a male reader. Sit back and relax while we read these beautiful stories out to you as you are about to go to sleep, while you're on a slow drive home from work or on a balcony with hot Camomile tea on a breezy, Saturday afternoon.

These audiobooks are available on our website as well as on international audiobook platforms.

www.ingramcontent.com/pod-product-compliance
Lightning Source LLC
Chambersburg PA
CBHW020316160726
47992CB00004B/1565